TEACH YOURSELF BOOKS

ENGLISH
GRAMMAR

Brian Phythian is Headmaster of Langley Park Boys' School, BeCkenham, Kent, and was previously Senior English Master of Manchester Grammar School. He is a graduate of the Universities of Oxford and Manchester, and a well-known writer on the teaching of English.

His books include four Concise Dictionaries: *Correct English, English Slang, English Idioms* and *Foreign Expressions,* all published by Hodder and Stoughton. He is also the author of *Help Your Child: Spelling*, editor of the Macmillan Shakespeare *Henry V*, and author and editor of a number of school textbooks in English language and literature.

ENGLISH GRAMMAR

B. A. Phythian M.A., M.Litt.

Hodder & Stoughton

A MEMBER OF THE HODDER HEADLINE GROUP

British Library Cataloguing in Publication Data

Phythian, B. A.
  English grammar.   Rev. Ed.
  (Teach yourself books)
  1. English language   Grammar   1950
  I. Title   II. Humphreys, Gordon.
  Teach yourself English grammar
  428.2   PE1112

ISBN 0 340 35873 4

First published 1980
Impression number   21   20
Year   1999   1998   1997

Printed in Great Britain for Hodder & Stoughton Educational,
a division of Hodder Headline plc, 338 Euston Road, London NW1 3BH
by Cox & Wyman Limited, Reading, Berks.

Contents

Acknowledgements

We are very grateful to the following for giving permission to quote extracts:

Gerald Durrell and Rupert Hart-Davis Limited/Granada Publishing Limited from *My Family and Other Animals*.

Laurie Lee and The Hogarth Press Limited from an adapted quote from *A Rose in Winter* (page 45 of the Penguin edition).

Eric Partridge and Hamish Hamilton Limited from an adapted quote from *Usage and Abusage* (©1965).

Simeon Potter and Penguin Books Limited from an adapted quote from *Our Language* (Pelican Original; revised edition, 1976; page 94; (© Simeon Potter, 1950, 1961, 1966 and 1976).

Preface

The original *Teach Yourself English Grammar*, by Gordon Humphreys, was published in 1945 and enjoyed considerable success. It adopted the conventional format of grammar books in devoting chapters to the principal parts of speech, and then dealing with the analysis of sentence-structure, including punctuation. Every piece of explanation was followed by exercises, the intention being that the student should be able to work his way through the book without any other aid.

When 1 was invited to revise the book, I was asked to retain this basic structure. The teaching of formal grammar in schools, and the testing of grammar in public examinations, have both declined, and have sometimes seemed in danger of disappearing, in favour of alternative, less structured (and by common consent less satisfactory) methods of teaching literacy and testing it. None the less, this book – however heavily revised and up-dated – continues to be based on the assumption that an understanding of the English Language must begin with a working knowledge of its components – the parts of speech – and with the way they fit together into the basic units of sense, notably the sentence. This knowledge is offered to the student not as an arid exercise, to enable him merely to distinguish a preposition from an adverb or a phrase from a clause, as a circus animal might jump through hoops, but as a means of gaining access to the richness and complexity of English expression, so as to be able to write and speak not only correctly but with variety, resourcefulness and, ultimately, elegance. This book sets out the first necessary stages; it is to be hoped that the student will find the confidence and encouragement to go much further.

B.A.P.

1   The Sentence

1   Phrases and sentences

A large part of our lives is spent in transferring our own thoughts
to other people. There are several ways in which we may do this.
We may express dislike by pulling a face; we may emit a sound
of pain if we are hurt; we may draw a map showing a friend the
way to a certain place. An artist may communicate through his
painting, and a composer through musical sounds. Diagrams,
road-signs and mathematical or scientific formulae are other
methods of communicating information or instruction.

The commonest way in which we express ourselves is, of
course, in words. The small child begins by making sounds, and
is then taught to say simple and single words, invariably to the
delight of adults. In the course of time, the child learns to communicate more complex thoughts or wishes by stringing several
words together, though often in a way that only the immediate
family can interpret. Finally, within a few years, the child can
frame sense-units that can be understood by all. Now he can talk
in *sentences*.

A sentence can be defined as a group of words making complete sense. This is not a full definition, as you will learn later,
but it will do for the moment. Not all groups of words make
sense. Consider

      (i) The at four o'clock is train next.
     (ii) Of the town they at the other side live.

If a person said this to us we could probably puzzle out what he meant, but he would not be speaking in sentences: he would be speaking a collection of words which have to be rearranged before they can be said to make sense.

However, these jumbles of words do contain smaller groups which do make sense; for example, *at four o'clock, of the town, at the other side*. But their sense is not complete; the words do not express a whole idea; they need other words to help them fit into an understandable statement. Such groups of words, making sense but not complete sense, are called *phrases*. Again you will find a fuller definition of *phrases* later in this book, but this definition will suffice for the present.

Now consider the following:

> (i) The next train is at four o'clock.
> (ii) They live at the other side of the town.

These groups of words make complete sense and express complete thoughts. They are sentences.

Exercise 1

State which of the following groups of words are sentences and which are not.

1. Huge fires were burning.
2. Thank you for your letter.
3. To comply with regulations.
4. The photograph is very blurred.
5. Spilt on the carpet.
6. On the fourth floor.
7. The next train is at four.
8. It may never happen.
9. Never on Sundays.
10. Without his knowledge.

Exercise 2

Construct sentences incorporating the following phrases (e.g. the phrase *at the match* could be part of the sentence *Forty thousand spectators were at the match*).

1. along the road 2. five pints of milk 3. together with all its contents 4. constructed in the early part of the sixteenth century 5. only a very few

2 The full stop and capital letter

If we wish to make more than one statement about an idea we are communicating, we may begin another sentence. If we make a statement and then go on to make a statement about something else, we begin another sentence. When speaking, people pause slightly between sentences, thus helping the listeners to follow the word-grouping being used. In writing, we avoid confusion between sentences by placing a full stop (.) at the end of each sentence and by beginning the following sentence with a capital letter.

Exercise 3

Full stops have been omitted from the following passages. Rewrite them, inserting a full stop at the end of each sentence and a capital letter at the beginning of the following one.

1. We reached the bus stop two old men stood there, not speaking, staring ahead down the road we stood behind them, and Father started to talk he was feeling very sad when the bus arrived, he seized my hand as it moved away I could see him through the steamed-up windows underneath the road bridge and towards the open fields the bus carried me away with increasing speed that was the last time I saw him.

2. We had a narrow escape a wave appeared high above the rest, and there was the usual moment of intense exertion it was of no use and in an instant the wave seemed to be hurling itself upon us with a yell of rage the steersman struggled with his oar to bring his prow to meet it he had almost succeeded when there was a crash and a rush of water round us I felt as if I had been struck upon the back with knotted ropes while foam gurgled round my knees and eyes.

3   Kinds of sentence

Notice the difference between the following sentences:

>   (i) We can't wait any longer.
>   (ii) Where are the scissors?
>   (iii) Keep off the grass.
>   (iv) What a nuisance it is!

The first of these sentences takes the form of a *statement*, the second is a *question*, the third is an order or *command*, and the fourth is an *exclamation*. All sentences take one of these four forms: statement, question, command (or request), or exclamation. Notice the appropriate punctuation (replacing the full stop) at the end of sentences 2 and 4.

Exercise 4

State whether the following sentences are statements, questions, commands (or requests) or exclamations.

1. Please pass the sugar.   2. How right you are!   3. Show me how you did it.   4. Travel is said to broaden the mind.   5. What time is it?   6. Get a move on.   7. What noisy neighbours you've got!   8. Who else is coming?   9. She asked for further details. 10. The crowd was ordered to disperse.

Exercise 5

Write three sentences (a statement, a question, a command) about each of the following words. For example, given the word *coal* one could write *Coal is an important natural resource* (statement), *What's the price of coal?* (question) and *Put some coal on the fire, please* (command/request).

1. door   2. cat   3. light

4 Parts of the sentence: subject and predicate

If you look at the sentence

> The museum is closed on Sundays.

you will see that it has two parts. The first part names what the sentence is about: *The museum*. The second part tells us something about *the museum*. Similarly, in the sentence

> The dog has chewed up my wallet.

we are told what the sentence is about (*The dog*) and then something about him (*chewed up my wallet*).

In both these sentences, the first part – that which names what we are thinking about in the sentence – is called *the subject*. The remainder of the sentence, making a statement about the subject, is called *the predicate*.

In every sentence, whether it is a statement, a question, a command or an exclamation, there is always a subject, naming the person or thing we are thinking about, and a predicate, which states what we are thinking about the subject.

Exercise 6

What is the subject of the following sentences?

1. An ambulance was soon on the scene. 2. You must be joking. 3. Despite the crowd, his voice could be clearly heard. 4. Wind and rain are forecast for tonight. 5. The weather-forecast promises wind and rain. 6. Throughout the day, news has been coming in about widespread flooding in East Anglia. 7. The rapidly falling birth-rate has taken planners by surprise. 8. The play was about the Russian Revolution.

5 Analysing a sentence

(a) In a sentence framed as a question, the order of words may be different from the normal order in a statement. For example,

You have travelled a long way. (statement)
Have you travelled a long way? (question)
Anyone can use it. (statement)
Can anyone use it? (question)

Nevertheless, the two essential parts of a sentence – subject and predicate – are there. In the first sentence, the subject is *You*; the subject of the second sentence is also *you*, even though it is no longer the first word in the sentence. In the third sentence, the subject is *Anyone*; the fourth sentence also has the subject *anyone*. If you are in doubt about the subject of a question, it is helpful to rephrase the question as a statement: the subject will usually become clearer then.

(*b*) In a sentence which has the form of a command or request, the subject is only rarely mentioned, but it is invariably *you*. When you see the 'command'

Fly to Canada by British Airways

or hear the instruction

Mind your step.

these mean

(You ought to) fly to Canada by British Airways.
(You must) mind your step.

In sentences of this kind, the subject is said to be *understood*: it is not actually stated in the sentence but is understood to be there. In both the above sentences the understood subject is *you*.

(*c*) In exclamations, the normal word order is often changed, as it is in questions:

How proud you must be!

means

You must be (how) proud.

and the subject is *you*.

(*d*) The word-order, then, is not necessarily a guide to the division of a sentence. The normal order is *subject* followed by *predicate*, but this order is frequently changed to give variety or emphasis to what is being expressed: this is specially true of poetry. When dealing with questions, commands and exclamations, you should mentally reconstruct them as statement-sentences before deciding what is the subject and what is the predicate. Thus

> Have you finished the job?
> Hurry along, please.
> What a tiring climb it is!

may be reconstructed as statements

> You have finished the job.
> (You must) hurry along please.
> It is (what) a tiring climb.

in a way which makes it clear that the subjects are *You*, *You* and *It*.

(*e*) Most of the illustrations used so far have consisted of very simple sentences (more complex ones will be described in later chapters) but you will already have realised that subjects and predicates can be quite lengthy. A simple sentence such as

> The dog curled up asleep

is analysed

Subject	Predicate
The dog	curled up asleep

But suppose the sentence reads

> The dog, worn out by his long walk, curled up asleep on the carpet in front of the fire.

Does *worn out by his long walk* tell us about *dog* or *curled up*? It describes *dog* and is therefore part of the subject. Does *on the carpet in front of the fire* tell us more about *dog* or more about *curled up*. It says *where* the curling up took place, and therefore belongs to the predicate.
The analysis is therefore

Subject	Predicate
The dog, worn out by his long walk	curled up on the carpet in front of the fire

Exercise 7

Divide the following into subject and predicate.

(*a*) *Statements*
1. The subject is not always the first word in a sentence.
2. They can't find it anywhere.
3. Never have I been more shocked.
4. The only way to learn how to spell correctly is to learn words by heart.

(*b*) *Questions*
5. Can anyone visit the castle?
6. What sort of car are you going to buy?
7. Who has been elected?
8. Has he been seen by a doctor?

(*c*) *Commands/requests*
9. Mind your head.
10. Ask that policeman.

(*d*) *Exclamations*
11. What a helpful man that was!
12. What an unpleasant experience she must have had!

(*e*) *Miscellaneous*
13. It's never easy to find your way there.
14. Come in.
15. What will be the outcome of the whole business?

Exercise 8

State whether the following are phrases or sentences. If they are sentences, state what sort.

1. Much official writing, such as routine letters to members of the public, explanatory circulars, and so on, needs merely to be clear, workmanlike and inoffensive.
2. With a tremendous amount of fuss and bother.
3. Be off!
4. Arriving precisely on time, for once.

5. I beg your pardon?
6. Don't worry.
7. A group of words making complete sense.
8. Good heavens, it's snowing!

Exercise 9

What are the subjects of the following sentences?

1. Be on the alert.
2. Among his most devoted admirers were the people from his native village.
3. The essential link between planning the use of the land and planning the necessary transport arrangements to enable people to get to the land in question was omitted.
4. Why did nobody warn him of the dangers?
5. It is very important to be able to understand the basic structure of a sentence.

2 The Noun

1 Parts of speech

For the purposes of studying language, all words may be placed in categories which are called 'parts of speech'. The main parts of speech are the noun, verb, adjective, pronoun, adverb, preposition and conjunction. The present chapter is concerned with the noun: the remaining parts of speech are dealt with in subsequent chapters.

2 Kinds of noun

A noun is a word which is the name of a person, place or thing, e.g. Shakespeare, Oxford, Spain, bicycle, rabbit, time, popularity, boy, luck, garden, opportunity.

There are four kinds or classes of nouns. The names of these classes need not be memorised, but they do help us to understand something of the wide variety of nouns.

(*a*)   Nouns which name particular people, places or things are called *proper nouns. Cleopatra* names a particular person, *Egypt* names a particular place, and *Cleopatra's Needle* in *London* is the name of a particular thing. All these are proper nouns. Proper nouns include the names of people, countries, cities, towns, villages, rivers, ships, streets, castles, mountains, months of the year, days of the week, festivals (*Christmas, Easter, New Year's*

Day) and particular names of institutions (*the United Nations, the British Broadcasting Corporation, the Royal Navy*) and firms (*British Petroleum, General Motors*).

Proper nouns always begin with capital letters.

(*b*) A noun which names a group of things regarded as a whole is called a *collective noun*. Examples of collective nouns include *forest, crowd, fleet, collection, team, congregation, jury, library*.

(*c*) An *abstract noun* is the name of a quality, state of mind, feeling or action. Abstract nouns refer to things which are intangible: *generosity, energy, attention, darkness, breadth, excellence, efficiency, science, rapidity, sin, criticism, health, anger, peace, choice, helpfulness, admiration*.

How many abstract nouns are there in the following sentence? Order, comfort, regularity, cheerfulness, good taste, pleasant conversation – these are the ornaments of daily life.

(*d*) Any noun which does not belong to one of the above three categories is called a *common noun*: a common noun is a name shared in common by everything of the same class or kind. Examples of common nouns include *book, bridge, wine, pen, water, taxi, glue, bird, woman, village*.

Exercise 10

In the following passages, the first nouns are in italics. Pick out the rest of the nouns.

1. We think of a *family* as consisting of a *father* and *mother* and their *children*. In African *societies*, usually the *children's children* are also included, and the whole family of fathers and mothers, uncles and aunts, brothers, sisters and cousins live close together, helping in the common concern for the provision of food and shelter. One member of the family helps another build his house or clear the brush for cultivation, just as one woman helps another hoe the fields. A hunter bringing back an antelope does not keep it for his wife and children alone, but divides it among these relatives

who have been less fortunate. In times of shortage, one relative can ask, and expect, help from another.

(*Colin Turnbull: adapted*)

2. I tend to stare when I am bored, and I am afraid I must have stared at that girl, without the least interest, a good deal. At any rate, I was certainly doing so at the moment when the strange experience began. Quite suddenly, without any faintness or nausea or any feeling of that sort, I found myself in a wholly different place. The familiar room vanished; Durward and Peggy vanished. I was alone. And I was standing up.

(*C. S. Lewis*)

3.   There was an old man of Blackheath
        Who sat on his set of false teeth.
            Said he, with a start,
            'O, Lord bless my heart,
        I have bitten myself underneath!'

4. We wish to apologise for the statement which appeared in last week's edition stating that Mr A. B. Smith is a defective in the local Police Force. We should, of course, have said that Mr Smith is a detective in the local Police Farce.

Exercise 11

Pick out the nouns in the following passages, stating whether they are proper, common, abstract or collective nouns.

1. Thus I got into my bones the essential structure of the ordinary British sentence – which is a noble thing. And when in my after years my schoolfellows who had won prizes and distinction for writing such beautiful Latin poetry and pithy Greek epigrams had come down again to common English, to earn their living or make their way, I did not feel myself at any disadvantage. Naturally I am biased in favour of boys learning English. I would make them all learn English: and then I would let the clever ones learn Latin as an honour, and Greek as a treat. But the only thing I would whip them

for is not knowing English. I would whip them hard for that.

(*Winston Churchill*)

2. Over the hill, the big flushed face of the moon poised just above the tree tops, very majestic, and far off – yet imminent. I turned with swift sudden friendliness to the net of elm-boughs spread over my head, dotted with soft clusters. I jumped up and pulled the cool soft tufts against my face for company; and as I passed, still I reached upwards for the touch of this budded gentleness of the trees. The wood breathed fragrantly, with a subtle sympathy.

(*D. H. Lawrence*)

Exercise 12

In each of the following groups of words, find the noun that belongs to a different category of noun from the rest.

1. convoy, fleet, flotilla, crew, men, unit.
2. joy, grief, tears, regret, endurance, despair.
3. peace, home, room, wife, chair, child.
4. Edinburgh, Fife, Scotland, Bruce, loch, Ben Nevis.

Exercise 13

What collective nouns are used to describe a collection of the following:

sheep, cattle, wolves, bees, lions, geese, young pigs, whales, teachers, singers, musicians, books, mountains, shrubs.

Exercise 14

Form abstract nouns from the following words:

selfish, cautious, polite, modest, scarce, coward, guilty, cruelly, brave, destroy, obey, choose, tempt, deduct.

3 Singular and plural

A noun is said to be *singular* (or *in the singular number*) if it refers to one thing: *wall, piece, property.*

A noun is said to be *plural* (or *in the plural number*) if it refers to more than one thing: *walls, pieces, properties.*

The plural of the majority of nouns is formed by adding -s to the singular form: *book, books*; *tie, ties*; *journey, journeys.*

The main exceptions to this rule are as follows:

(*a*) Nouns ending in a hissing sound add -es, not -s: *ash, ashes*; *fox, foxes*; *dress, dresses.* This applies to nouns ending in -s, -sh, -ch (soft sound), -x, -z, -o. Thus *loss, losses*; *parish, parishes*; *match, matches*; *fox, foxes*; and the commonly mis-spelt *potato-es, tomato-es.* However, some words that end in -o and are of foreign origin form their plurals in the normal way: *solo-s, oratorio-s, canto-s, folio-s, piano-s, proviso-s, cameo-s, tyro-s.* Words ending in -is have -es in the plural: *crisis, crises*; *oasis, oases.*

(*b*) Nouns ending in -f and -fe form the plural by changing -f, -fe into -ves: *knife, knives*; *half, halves.* However, some words ending in -f form the plural in the normal way: *chief-s, dwarf-s, gulf-s, grief-s, proof-s, reef-s.* A few nouns have two plural forms: *wharfs, wharves*; *scarfs, scarves*; *hoofs, hooves.*

(*c*) Some nouns have irregular plurals: *child, children*; *ox, oxen*; *man, men*; *mouse, mice*; *foot, feet*; *goose, geese*; *tooth, teeth.*

(*d*) A noun which ends with a -y preceded by a consonant changes the -y into -ies: *ally, allies*; *country, countries*; *reply, replies.* However, nouns ending in -y preceded by a vowel follow the normal rule: *ray, rays*; *jersey, jerseys*; *toy, toys.*

(*e*) Some nouns have the same form in the plural as in the singular: *sheep, swine, deer, salmon, cod, trout.*

(*f*) Some nouns of foreign origin retain their foreign plurals: *phenomenon, phenomena*; *addendum, addenda*; *datum, data*; *radius, radii.* However, if a foreign word becomes very popular, it may have an 'English' plural as well as the original foreign one. Thus *automaton* may have either *automatons* or *automata*, and *memorandum* may have *memorandums* or *memoranda* (but never *memorandas*).

Irregular plurals of this kind are usually recorded in dictionaries, and only (*a*), (*b*) and (*d*) above are worth memorising.

There are some other peculiarities of the plural:

(*a*) Some nouns, because of their meaning, have no singular form, only a plural one: *trousers, scissors, dregs, mathematics, measles,* etc. Words such as *news, politics* and *mathematics* are curious because they are plural words used as if they were singular: *The news is* (not *are*) *good. Politics is a dirty business.*

(*b*) Some nouns may change their meanings when they appear in the plural: *manner, manners; compass, compasses; spectacle, spectacles; spirit, spirits; brace, braces.*

(*c*) A few nouns have two plural forms with different meanings: *staff, staffs* (groups of employees), *staves* (clubs or sticks); *genius, geniuses* (very clever people), *genii* (spirits); *cloth, cloths, clothes.*

(*d*) If a noun consists of several words, the -s is added to the important one: *daughters-in-law; courts-martial; lookers-on.* But note *cupfuls, basketfuls.*

Exercise 15

Using the above rules, give the plurals of the following:

valley, victory, business, wife, army, cargo, rush, chimney, loaf, watch, life, sixty, dish, potato, hoax, window, bus, essay, brass, cliff, teaspoonful, passer-by, basis.

4 Gender

Those of you who have studied a foreign language will know that in some languages nouns are described as being 'masculine' or 'feminine', as in French, or additionally 'neuter', as in German. In French, for instance, a town is feminine (*une ville*) but a village is masculine (*un village*). It will be clear from this example that these categories, which are called *genders*, have nothing to do with sex.

Gender is of little or no importance in English, though it will be found referred to in old grammar books. For example, such common words as *the* and *a* do not have different forms depending on whether the following noun is masculine or feminine, as they do in some European languages. For all practical purposes, the general reader may forget all about gender.

A few English nouns can be said to have both masculine and feminine forms to indicate sex: *hero*, *heroine*; *manager*, *manageress*; *widower*, *widow*. Most English nouns, however, have completely different forms for the sexes: *boy*, *girl*; *king*, *queen*; *dog*, *bitch*. Some nouns refer to either sex: *friend*, *cousin*, *neighbour*.

A personal interest in a thing which is inanimate may cause it to be regarded as feminine; thus a sailor may speak of his ship, or a motorist of his car, as *she* or *her*. Conversely, while a family will speak of a pet as *he/him* or *she/her* depending on the animal's sex, it is equally correct to refer to an animal as *it*.

5   Possession

Examine these sentences:

> The passengers were becoming impatient.
> The passenger's ticket was invalid.
> The passengers' waiting-room was full.

In the first sentence, *passengers* is the straightforward plural of the noun *passenger*, and denotes that more than one passenger was becoming impatient. In the second sentence, the word *passenger's* indicates that the ticket belonged to one passenger. In the third sentence, *passengers'* denotes that the waiting-room was for more than one passenger. The forms *passenger's* and *passengers'* denote ownership or possession: these forms are described grammatically as being in the *possessive* (or *genitive*) *case*.

The normal way of expressing possession is by the use of the *apostrophe*, a raised comma ('), though there are other ways, e.g.

The ticket *of the passenger* was invalid.

The waiting-room *for passengers* was full.

The general rule is to add-'s to singular words, and an apostrophe without the -s to plural words:

The boy's hand was hurt (i.e. the hand of one *boy*).

The shop sells boys' clothes (i.e. clothes for *boys*).

The lady's face was red with exertion.

Ladies' fashions have changed little this year.

But there is one very important exception to this rule: if a plural noun does not end in -s, the possessive is formed by adding -'s, even though the word is plural. Thus: *children's games, women's liberation, policemen's responsibilities.*

Which is correct: *men's trousers* or *mens' trousers*? The meaning is *trousers for men*; the operative noun is *men*; it does not end in -s, so the possessive is formed in the normal way by adding -'s; *men's trousers* is therefore correct.

There is an occasional complication in the case of proper nouns ending in -s, such as *Charles, Dickens, James.* If it is necessary to use such words in the possessive, either form of the possessive is correct, i.e.

Charles' reign *or* Charles's reign

Dickens' novels *or* Dickens's novels

St James' life *or* St James's life

The simpler version, using the apostrophe without the -s, is usually preferred. Likewise, note that *for goodness' sake* is irregularly punctuated, on the grounds that people do not normally say *for goodness's sake* with three consecutive -s sounds. Other information about the possessive case may be found in Chapter 5.

Exercise 16

Write out the following, putting one word in the possessive case (e.g. The leg of the dog – The dog's leg):

1. The reach of a man.   2. The best friend of a boy.   3. The den

of lions.   4. The achievements of men.   5. Clothes of women.
6. The lid of the box.   7. The sleeves of the dress.   8. The cost
of the dresses.

Exercise 17

The following examples of the possessive case are in the singular.
Put them into the plural:

1. The boy's possessions.   2. The child's hobbies.   3. The
country's exports.   4. Man's aspirations.   5. The sheep's
safety.   6. A woman's place.   7. The team's results.   8. The
army's exercises.

6   Use of the dictionary

There are some nouns of which the pronounciation is identical
with, or very similar to, that of other words which, however, have
a different meaning and spelling. For example, there are important differences between *stationary* and *stationery*, *complement*
and *compliment*, *recourse* and *resource*, *practice* and *practise*.

Exercise 18

In the following sentences, locate the word wrongly used, and
supply the correct one.
1. The office of the college Principle is on the first floor.   2. The
caste included Laurence Olivier.   3. He can play only a few
cords on the guitar.   4. The play is full of illusions to contemporary life.   5. Extracts from the book have already appeared in
cereal form. 6. He was wearing a three-piece suite.   7. Every
chorister was wearing a clean surplus.   8. The tax changes take
affect next September.   9. There was thunder and lightening all
night.   10. The postman's daughter sorts out the male.

Revision

Exercise 19

Divide into subject and predicate.

1. The next train is due in twenty minutes. 2. Come into the garden. 3. What can be more enjoyable than a long swim on a hot summer's day? 4. Shall we have another attempt? 5. I can actually write my name in the dust on the table. 6. You must be joking. 7. What did he say? 8. The next opportunity for promotion will not occur until next year.

Exercise 20

Give the plurals of the following, using a dictionary if necessary:

monkey, pony, woman, cod, library, sheaf, contralto, march, waltz, motto, analysis, roof, memorandum, on-looker, ring-side seat, belief, thief, loaf, aquarium, premium, handkerchief, bus, criterion, himself, commander-in-chief.

Exercise 21

Give six examples of nouns which are used only in the plural.

Exercise 22

Turn back to the list of nouns whose plural forms have different meanings from the singular forms. Say what is the difference of meaning in each case.

Exercise 23

Give the feminine equivalent of:

monk, bachelor, lord, widower, drake, masseur, student, duke.

Exercise 24

Form abstract nouns from the following words:

wise, deep, excite, confident, delicate, rotate, adjust, capable, eager, disobey.

Exercise 25

Supply a synonym (a word having the same meaning) and an antonym (a word have the opposite meaning) for the following nouns: e.g. enthusiasm (synonym, *zeal*; antonym, *apathy*):

prosperity, fatigue, strength, generosity, gentleness, courage, contentment, monotony, agreement, sympathy.

Exercise 26

Insert apostrophes in the following:

It is not true that the French live on frogs legs. Their chefs training is so thorough that French cooking is extremely varied. Lorry drivers tastes are such that transport cafes have excellent menus. Englands standards, especially on motorways, leave much to be desired. Years of progress will be needed before our catering can challenge Frances.

Exercise 27

Pick out the nouns in the following, stating whether they are common, collective, abstract or proper:

I am very sensitive to observation, and often have this feeling not only in the presence of human beings but in that of small animals. Once I even traced the source of it to a large spider whose mysterious eyes were fixed upon me. I now began to search around to see what it could be that was looking at me. Eventually I came upon a set of masks, whose slanting eyes were turned mournfully in my direction. I examined them with care and was struck by the unnerving beauty of their design.

One or two of them distantly reminded me of Indian Buddahs I had seen. I found them very alarming objects indeed, and put them down nervously after a little while.

(Iris Murdoch: adapted)

Exercise 28

Write down, as fully as you can,

1. The rules for forming the plural in English
2. the rules for using the apostrophe to express possession
3. the definition of the four classes of noun.

Then check the accuracy and completeness of what you have written by referring to the chapter.

3   The Adjective

1   Adding to the meaning

To walk into a shoe-shop and ask the assistant for a pair of shoes is to present him with a considerable problem, given that there are probably thousands of pairs of shoes in the shop. If, in answer to his 'What sort of shoes?', one answers '*Brown*', the problem is immediately much reduced. Further information such as '*Plain*' or '*Cheap*' limits the choice still further. By the time one has added '*square-toed*', '*rubber-soled*' or '*high-heeled*', the description may be precise enough for the assistant to begin to select a manageable number for the customer to choose from.

Words that add something to the meaning of a noun and limit its sense in this way are called *adjectives*. The italicised words in the previous paragraph are all adjectives (*brown, plain, cheap*), some of them being adjectives formed from words which can act as other parts of speech (*square-toed, rubber-soled, high-heeled*). The word *square* can be a noun (*I will meet you in the square*) as well as an adjective (*a square garden*); *toe* is a noun; *square-toed* is an adjective. *Rubber* can be a noun (*Rubber is extracted from trees*) or an adjective (*rubber tyres*); *sole* can be a noun (*the sole of a shoe*) or, in a different sense, an adjective (*my sole reason for coming*); *rubber-soled* is an adjective. All the italicised words in the first paragraph of this section are adjectives capable of being applied to the noun *shoes*.

The simple definition of an adjective is that it is a word that describes a noun (or pronoun: see Chapter 6). Adjectives sharpen a picture as a photographer focuses a lens. They add precision to speech or writing: they add beauty, power and reality to literature.

Whether a word is an adjective or not depends on its *function* in a sentence. A person may be an *invalid* (noun): a vote may be *invalid* (adjective). The pronunciation helps in this case, but it may not always do so: one may enjoy a *sound* sleep (adjective), not making a *sound* (noun).

Exercise 29

Pick out the adjectives in the following:

The huge drums rolled. Great fires leaped up. Massive engines crawled across the wide field. In the midst was a mighty battering-ram, fifty feet in length, on thick chains. It had been forged in dark smithies, and its hideous head, of black steel, was shaped like a fierce wolf.

2 Position of adjectives

If an adjective is used to describe a noun, it is normally placed before the noun: a *quick* answer, the *rough* surface, *several new* designs. Other positions are possible: The music, though *pleasant*, lacks interest; The farm-house, *deserted* and *dilapidated*, is likely to be demolished.

Adjectives are often used to complete a predicate when a sentence would fail to make sense without one: The strawberries taste *sweet*; The sky grew *red*.

Exercise 30

Supply adjectives appropriate to the following nouns:

reasons, doctor, dog, shower, manners, decision, menu, seats, policy, noise.

Exercise 31

Complete the predicate by adding suitable adjectives:

The spectators were ... The sea became ... Danger seemed ...
The water feels ... The policeman looked ... The wine
tastes ... The bread is not ... The confusion was made ...

3 Kinds of adjectives

Adjectives add to the meaning of nouns in different ways. The
most common describe some *quality*, which a person or thing
may have: *brown* shoes, a *silly* question, *dangerous* driving.

Other adjectives may describe *quantity*. The quantity referred
to may be precise (*thirty thousand* visitors, the *fourth* telephone
call) or indefinite (*many* enquiries, *several* times).

A small group of adjectives denotes possession: *my* pen, *your*
opinion, *his* secretary, *her* tastes, *its* wheels, *our* mistake, *their*
friends. (In Chapter 6 these italicised words will be more accur-
ately defined as pronouns in the possessive case, but for the
moment they may be regarded as adjectives.)

Another small group consists of *demonstrative* adjectives,
pointing out something: *this* card, *that* shelf, *these* tools, *those*
numbers.

Adjectives may be *interrogative*, asking a question: *Which* way
are you going? *What* plans have you made? *Whose* diary is this?
Such words are adjectives only if they have a noun to describe.
The interrogative words in the following sentences are not adjectives: *What* did he say? *Why* are we waiting? *When* will it be
finished? These words, and other similar ones, will be explained
in a later chapter.

Finally, adjectives may be *emphatic* (my *own* work), *distributive* (*each* person, *every* occasion) or *exclamatory* (*what* courage!).

There is no need to memorise these categories, which are
mentioned merely to indicate the range of adjectival functions.
It is only necessary to be able to distinguish adjectives from
other parts of speech.

Exercise 32

With the help of the above definitions, identify the adjectives in the following.

Penguins are notorious thieves and are not able to look after their own property for a long time. There is endless robbery always going on in each rookery. One who spent much time watching the habits of these birds said he saw a cock-penguin working with great diligence, stealing many stones from neighbouring nests to make his own. But as soon as he turned to fetch more stones, another rascally thief would come along, stand by the nest for a few minutes, as if uninterested in the nest-building. Suddenly it would dart, seize the nearest stone and make off. What action did the hen take? She looked on while her own home was robbed before her very eyes, as if she did not understand what was happening. When the cock returned, he made up for his recent loss by a thieving expedition to another nest.

4 Adjectives in comparisons

Consider these sentences:

> Ben Nevis is a *high* mountain.
> Mont Blanc is a *higher* mountain.
> Mount Everest is the *highest* mountain.

In the first sentence, *high* is simply an adjective expressing a quality of the mountain. In the second sentence, *higher* is an adjective used to compare Mont Blanc with Ben Nevis. Mont Blanc is the higher of the two mountains. In the third sentence, *highest* is used to compare Everest with all other mountains. The comparison here is not of two mountains but of more than two.

These three forms, *high, higher, highest*, are examples of what are called the degrees of comparison. *High* is the ordinary form of the adjective (called the *positive degree*, though the name need not be memorised). *Higher* is called the *comparative degree*, which is the form of the adjective used when two things or people are being compared. *Highest* is called the *superlative degree*, which is the form of the adjective used when something or someone is superior to all others in the particular quality denoted by the adjective.

Short words, like *high*, form the comparative degree by adding -er and the superlative by adding -est. Thus *small, smaller, smallest; cold, colder, coldest; fast, faster, fastest; short, shorter, shortest*. In some words, the final consonant is doubled before the -er and -est: *thin, thinner, thinnest; fat, fatter, fattest; big bigger, biggest*. Another rule is that when an adjective ends with a -y with a consonant in front, the -y changes into -i before the -er and -est; *happy, happier, happiest; dry, drier, driest*. If the adjective ends with a -y with a vowel in front, however, the -y remains unchanged before the -er and -est endings: *grey, greyer, greyest*.

With long words, it is usual to form the comparative and superlative by using *more* and *most*: *energetic, more energetic, most energetic; beautiful, more beautiful, most beautiful; rapid, more rapid, most rapid*.

Some of the most common adjectives have irregular degrees of comparison:

good	better	best
bad	worse	worst
little	less	least
much/many	more	most

The superlative form of an adjective is sometimes used not for the purpose of direct comparison, but simply for emphasis:

He was given a *most cordial* welcome.

This does not necessarily imply that the welcome was the most cordial imaginable, or the most cordial he had ever received; the superlative form merely stresses the high degree of the quality of the adjective *cordial*.

Owing to their meaning, some adjectives have no degrees of comparison, strictly speaking. If your garden is *more square* than your neighbour's, then his cannot be square in the first place. This is something of a quibble with words like *round, universal* and *perfect*, but the word *unique* is often misused in this way. Something is either *unique* or it is not: there cannot be degrees of uniqueness.

Exercise 33

Give the comparative and superlative of the following:

kind, benevolent, loving, good, pure, holy, innocent, careless, hard, cruel, evil, bad, small, little, tiny, late, far, silly, gay, out, lively.

5 Correct constructions

(*a*) It must be remembered that when two things or persons are being compared, the comparative is used, not the superlative:

Which is the *older* building, St Paul's Cathedral or Westminster Abbey? (not *oldest*)

Which of the two routes is (the) *quicker*? (not *quickest*).

It is a very common error to use the superlative when only two things or persons are being compared:

Of the cup-finalists, Manchester United have been the *most* successful in recent months. (Should be *more*, there being only two teams in a cup-final.)

Conversely, the superlative must be used of more than two:

Who is the oldest of your three children? (not *older*).

(*b*) In the sentence

He is *more skilful* than the whole of the team.

the comparative is loosely used. How can he be more skilful than a group of people of whom he is one? A comparative can be used only to compare one thing or person with something or someone separate from itself. The sentence should read

He is more skilful than the rest of the team.

(*c*) Note the following example of an error in the use of the superlative:

John is the tallest of his brothers.

John cannot be the tallest of a group to which he does not belong: he is not one of *his brothers*. Just as London cannot be the largest of the American cities, and Wordsworth cannot be the best of French poets, John cannot be the tallest of his brothers, because he is not one of his brothers.

The sentence should read

> John is the tallest of *the* brothers.

or

> John is taller than his brothers.

(*d*)   One often hears such sentences as

> I don't like those kind of films.

Note that *kind* is a singular noun. It therefore should have a singular adjective. *Those* is a plural adjective; the correct singular form is *that*:

> I don't like *that kind* of films.

or

> I don't like *those kinds* of films.

Similar errors are found with other collective nouns, such as *class* and *type*. Care should be taken to avoid such inaccuracies as *these class, those type*.

Exercise 34

Correct the following:

1. Our MP is reputed to be a better speaker than all the members of the House of Commons.
2. House prices are now the highest they have ever been before.
3. He of all others should have been the most careful.
4. This was the biggest shock we had ever suffered before.
5. The United States has perhaps the greatest natural resources of all other countries.
6. I think he is the best of the two at darts.
7. To attack was more preferable than to withdraw.
8. As far as the eighteenth and nineteenth centuries are concerned, the latter showed the greatest industrial advancement.
9. The painted ceiling is a very unique feature.
10. The painted ceiling is almost unique.
11. These kind of toys are very dangerous.
12. I prefer those sort of flowers.

6 Adjectival equivalents

(*a*)   Sometimes a word that is usually used as a noun functions as an adjective: *summer* dresses, *apple* pie, *garden* tools. Even though a word may normally be a noun, if it is used to describe another noun it is an adjective.

(*b*)   A group of words, which may or may not contain an adjective, may do the work of an adjective. One may refer to *the shop at the corner* or to *the corner shop*. The phrase *at the corner* is adjectival. Likewise one may describe someone as a *promising* athlete (using an adjective, *promising*) or as an athlete *of promise* (using an adjectival phrase, *of promise*).

Exercise 35

Write sentences using the following nouns as adjectives:

tennis, book, floor, chalk, grass, door, bread, pig.

Exercise 36

Replace the adjectival phrases (italicised) by adjectives.

1. His reply was *to the point*.
2. The damage was *beyond repair*.
3. It was a decision *agreed to without exception*.
4. He is a person *inclined to believe everything*.
5. The scientists enjoyed success *at the outset*.
6. Make sure you are *on time*.
7. He has made a special study of life *under the sea*.
8. It is a substance *easily set on fire*.

Exercise 37

Replace the adjectives by adjectival phrases.

1. The distant hills were covered in haze.

2.   He has a ginger-haired sister.
3.   You are too gullible.
4.   They enjoy a carefree life.
5.   Her skill at gymnastics is almost incredi le.

7   The definite and indefinite articles

The word *the* is called the *definite article* because it indicates a particular person or thing. The words *a* and *an* are the *indefinite articles* because they do not denote a particular person or thing. The indefinite article *a* is used before a word beginning with a consonant or consonant sound, and *an* is used before a word beginning with a vowel (*a, e, i, o, u*) or vowel sound. Thus

> *a* corner
> *an* unlucky accident

but

> *a* university

because though *university* begins with a vowel, it is pronounced 'you-niversity' as if it began with a consonant; i.e. it begins with a consonant sound. Other words which begin with a vowel pronounced as a consonant include *union, once, unit, European.* Words which begin with a consonant but which are pronounced as if they began with a vowel include *honest, honour, hour,* etc., where the *h* is silent. Thus *an hour's journey, an honorary secretary*, etc.

When two or more adjectives describe the same noun, or when two nouns are closely associated, only one article is necessary:

> a black and white frock
> the rights and wrongs of the matter

If you pack a *black and white frock*, you pack one frock; if you pack *a black and a white frock*, you pack two frocks, one white and one black. If you order *a vodka and lemonade*, you order one drink; if you order *a vodka and a lemonade*, you order two drinks.

The word *the* is both singular and plural (the *taxi*, the *taxis*), but *a* and *an* are singular only, the plural being *some*, which may be omitted:

Would you like a potato?
Would you like some potatoes?

or simply

Would you like potatoes?

8 Miscellaneous

(*a*) The adjective *few* can be used in three ways:
I spent *a few* days abroad.   (i.e. a small number)
I spent *few* days abroad.   (i.e. not many, scarcely any)
I spent *the few* days of my holiday building a greenhouse.
   (i.e. all there were)
It must be remembered that *few*, *fewer*, *fewest* are used of numbers, and that *little*, *less*, *least* are used of quantity. The words *fewer* and *less* are often wrongly used. Examples of correct use: *less* expense, *fewer* expenses; *less* trouble, *fewer* troubles; *less* chance, *fewer* chances. It is worth remembering that *less* is used with a singular noun and *fewer* with a plural one.

(*b*) There is a tendency for some adjectives to be grossly overworked. It is easy to use a simple and handy adjective when a little thought would suggest a more appropriate, distinctive or precise one which would give more interest and colour to one's expression. To young people, much is *fantastic* or simply *great*; to footballers all refereeing is *diabolical*; the weather is invariably either *nice* or *awful*.
She is in bed with a *bad* leg. It is particularly *bad* in *bad* weather, and makes her *bad*-tempered because she has *bad* nights. She's also a very *bad* patient, and gives her daughter a *bad* time.
This could be made less monotonous and more precise:
She is in bed with an *arthritic* (etc.) leg. It is particularly *painful* in *wet* (etc.) weather, and makes her *irritable* because she has *disturbed* nights. She's also a very *difficult* patient and makes demands on her daughter.

Exercise 38

Insert either *less* or *fewer*:

1. There is ... opportunity for study. 2. ... babies were born last year. 3. It would be more comfortable if there were ... people. 4. There are ... salmon in the stream than there used to be. 5. Since she got married we have had ... news from her.

Exercise 39

Substitute better adjectives in the following:

1. a nice holiday, a nice boy, a nice smile, a nice smell.
2. nasty weather, nasty experience, nasty behaviour, nasty day.
3. awful noise, awful crowds, awful driving conditions, awful shame.

Revision

Exercise 40

Write out definitions of the following, and then check the accuracy of what you have written by referring to the above chapter:

adjective; comparative; superlative; definite and indefinite articles.

Exercise 41

Give the adjectives formed from the following proper nouns:

Holland, Norway, Spain, Switzerland, Sweden, Cuba, Peru, Paris, Naples, Vienna, Christ, Buddha, Caesar, Napoleon, Shakespeare, Shaw.

Exercise 42

Give the adjectives formed from the following nouns:

event, home, talk, moment, mood, demon, serpent, burden, crisis, control, reality, god.

Exercise 43

Use a dictionary to find the differences between the following pairs of adjectives:

respectful, respectable; official, officious; luxurious, luxuriant; contemptuous, contemptible; incredulous, incredible; graceful, gracious; credible, creditable; uninterested, disinterested; legible, eligible; judicial, judicious.

Exercise 44

Give an adjective opposite in meaning (i.e. an antonym):

learned, dull, virtuous, industrious, hostile, transitory.

Exercise 45

Correct the following:

1. We have had less apples from the trees this year.
2. Those type of clothes are becoming very fashionable.
3. Which is the cheapest of the two?
4. He seems disinterested in his work.
5. Lead-mining is the village's principle industry.

4 The Verb

1 Definition

In Chapter 1, it was explained that all sentences can be divided into two parts, subject and predicate. The word or group of words forming the subject states what the sentence is about. The rest of the sentence – the predicate – makes a statement about the subject. Examine the following sentences:

(i) The conjurer produced a rabbit from the hat.
(ii) All pupils in English schools attend until shortly after their sixteenth birthday.

In the first sentence, the subject is *The conjurer*: in the second sentence it is *All pupils in English schools*. The subject is often first in the sentence, but not always: note the subjects (italicised) in

(iii) At the beginning of this book is *a list of contents*.
(iv) Where were *you*?

If you now look back at the predicates in the four sentences quoted, you will see that in every case there is one word which tells us what the subject actually did. The conjurer *produced*; all pupils *attend*; a list of contents *is*; you *were* somewhere. These italicised words are, structurally or grammatically, the most important words in the sentences because they are the words that make statements about the subjects; they tell us what actually happened. They are called verbs. In the first two sentences, the verbs (*produced, attend*) express action. In the other two sentences the verbs (*is, were*) express being. *A verb denotes action or being.* All sentences must contain a verb with a subject.

Exercise 46

Pick out the verbs in the following:

1. Another coal barge passed us, low in the water. 2. The chug of its engine was now the only sound on the river. 3. It pushed the water aside as if it was only a rubber sheet. 4. There were two white gulls above the brown foam. 5. He looked across the river at the different coloured wool bales. 6. They overflowed from their big wooden trolleys. 7. I stayed and talked to the stockyard clerk about his pigeons until the buzzer went. 8. Was he happy?

2 Subject of verbs

The grammatical term *subject* can now be defined in more detail as the word or group of words performing the action or state of being denoted in the verb. To identify the subject, locate the verb and then pick out what it is that performs the action of the verb. The subjects of the following sentences are italicised:

I feel unwell.
The miles and miles of sand, with their pools, rocks and wild high cliffs attract many holiday-makers.
Have *we* enough time?
Despite the bad weather and the danger of flooding, *the search* continues.

In some grammar books, words acting as the subject of a verb are said to be *in the subjective case* or *in the nominative case*.

Many sentences, of course, have more than one verb, but these will be dealt with later.

Frequently the verb consists of a single word, as in all the examples quoted so far. Very often, however, the verb consists of two, three or even more words:

> The referee *postponed* the match.
> The match *was postponed*.
> It *has been postponed*.
> It *should have been postponed*.

There is still only one verb in these sentences, even though it may comprise several words. Occasionally, a word may be interposed between the words that make up the verb

> I *have* nearly *exhausted* my supply of matches.
> *Have* you *seen* him recently?

The verbs here are *have exhausted* and *have seen*.

Exercise 47

What is the subject of the following sentences?

1. We reached the summit of a hill.   2. A light fall of snow remained from the previous night.   3. A faint sun struggled through the bare branches of the lifeless trees.   4. Under the thin snow, brown earth and dark grass showed through.   5. Was spring far away?

Exercise 48

Identify the verbs in the following.

1. I am really a foreigner.   2. I married when I was twenty and the only reason I came to this village was that there was a house at the right price.   3. We didn't move here at once because I was still a student.   4. If we had moved to a town, it would have meant a high rent.   5. Has the village always been like this? 6. City life would never have suited us.   7. We should probably have felt overcrowded.   8. How can people ever survive in such an atmosphere?   9. When I am at work, it is this house I constantly think of.   10. There is a real sense of community here.

Exercise 49

Divide these sentences into subject and predicate.

1. The two prisoners had nothing in common. 2. The Bishop was a slight wisp of a man in his fifties, with a touch of the peasant about him. 3. The Mayor, a great bull of a man with angry eyes, had stiff black hair. 4. How could such a strange pair have come together? 5. The General's face could have been that of a thoughtful scholar.

3   Object of verbs

Consider the sentence
> Fire destroyed the house.

There are three ideas here: (i) *Fire*, the doer of the action; (ii) *destroyed*, the verb which states the action; (iii) *the house*, which receives or suffers the action.

Fire is the subject of the verb *destroyed*; *the house* is said to be the *object* of the verb *destroyed*.

Any word or group of words that receives or suffers the action described in a verb is said to be the object of that verb. In some grammar books, words which are the object of a verb are said to be *in the objective case* or *in the accusative case*.

When a verb has an object, it is said to be *transitive* (from the Latin *trans*, meaning *across*, as in *trans-Atlantic*). In the sentence
> Fire destroyed the house

the action of the verb *destroyed* is 'carried across' from the subject to the object; *destroyed* in this sentence is a transitive verb.

To locate the object of a verb, find the verb and ask whether there are any words on which the action of the verb is carried out.

Exercise 50

Pick out the objects in the following sentences:

1. They found a few empty bottles. 2. He has hurt his knee.
3. I do not like that colour. 4. He has spilt his tea. 5. They
have explored the South Atlantic. 6. I will not permit that.
7. That I will not permit. 8. What have you found? 9.
Which did you choose? 10. Whose letter shall we reply to
first?

4 Intransitive verbs

Consider the sentence
                    Wood floats but iron sinks.
There are two verbs in this sentence, *floats* and *sinks*. The
subject of the former is *wood*, and of the latter *iron*. Neither verb
has an object; the actions of the verbs are complete in themselves;
there is no 'carrying across'.

When a verb denotes an action that is complete in itself, the
verb is said to be *intransitive*.

It is possible for a verb to be intransitive in some uses, and
transitive in others. For instance, *sinks* is intransitive in the example already quoted, but transitive in the headline
                    Explosion sinks oil-tanker.
Other examples of verbs used both transitively and intransitively:
        I shall return your book next week. (transitive)
        I shall return tomorrow. (intransitive)
        The team lost. (intransitive)
        She has lost her cheque book. (transitive)
To ascertain whether a verb is transitive or intransitive,
mentally place *what?* or *whom?* after the verb: if the answer to
the question can be supplied from the sentence, the verb is
transitive. If no answer can be provided *from the sentence* the
verb is intransitive. Thus

All the competitors *finished* the race. *Finished* what? Answer –
the race. Therefore the verb *finished* is transitive: it has an
object.

All the competitors *finished* before nightfall. *Finished* what? No answer is given in the sentence, so *finished* is here intransitive.

The news *cheered* him. *Cheered* whom? Answer – *him*.

The verb is transitive.

The spectators *cheered* with great enthusiasm. *Cheered* whom or what?

No answer. Intransitive verb.

Exercise 51

Say whether the verbs in the following sentences are transitive or intransitive.

1. Please write. 2. Please write a letter. 3. The incoming tide rocked the boat. 4. The boat rocked gently at its moorings. 5. Jump! 6. Jump quickly! 7. They've jumped the queue. 8. Don't cross the road. 9. Don't cross until I tell you. 10. What shall I pack? 11. When shall we pack?

Exercise 52

Compose sentences using the following words, first transitively and then intransitively: e.g. We *turned* the corner (transitive); The tide *has turned* (intransitive).

hear, talk, move, wave, win, write, recover, rest, melt, drive.

5 The indirect object

Some verbs may be followed by two objects:

> I asked *him* the *reason*.
> Tell *me* the *truth*.

These mean

> I asked (*from*) *him* the reason.
> Tell (*to*) *me* the truth.

The object of the first verb is *the reason*, and of the second *the truth*. The words *him* and *me* are called indirect objects.

See also Chapter 10, section 3.

Exercise 53

Pick out the indirect objects.

1. Give him the keys. 2. He showed them the garden. 3. Throw the dog a biscuit. 4. Please hand me that paint-brush. 5. We have bought them a wedding present.

6. Verbs of incomplete predication

So far we have seen that the predicate of a sentence may consist of

(*a*)   a transitive verb with its object:

He/*tested the tyres by kicking them.*

(*b*)   an intransitive verb, with or without other words in the predicate:

The snow/ *has melted.*

Rain/ *fell during the night, but not very heavily.*

Some intransitive verbs, however, cannot form a predicate by themselves. They always need another word, or several words, to complete the predicate. For example, *The day was.* does not make complete sense, and so is not a grammatical sentence: *was* cannot form a predicate on its own, and needs some other word(s) (*sunny, nearly over, the most unpleasant one of the entire holiday*) to complete the sense. The most common verb of this type is the verb *to be* with all its parts (e.g. *am, are, is, was, were, will* (*be*), *shall* (*be*)). Others include *become* and *seem*:

He/ became Chancellor of the Exchequer.

The villagers/ seemed very helpful.

These predicative words which are needed to complete the sense of such verbs are called the *complement*. In other words, such verbs cannot take an object: they are intransitive verbs needing a complement (i.e. something to complete them).

Exercise 54

Pick out the complements.

1. It is his birthday next Saturday. 2. They do not seem friendly. 3. He turned informer. 4. With a little practice you will become experts. 5. This was our first choice. 6. They must have been the last to arrive. 7. Vaduz is the capital of Lichtenstein. 8. What is the capital of Luxembourg?

7   Person

You will have noticed that English verbs change their form in certain circumstances: I *am* happy, you *are* happy, he *is* happy. Likewise

> The car *has* arrived.
> The cars *have* arrived.

but

> There *goes* the fire-engine.

but

> There *go* the fire-engines.

These changes in form depend on what is called the *person* of the verb. There are three persons, each of them having a singular and plural, as follows:

First Person: a verb is in the first person singular if the subject is *I*, and the first person plural if the subject is *we. We* is plural of *I*.

Second Person: a verb is in the second person if the subject is *you*. The second person forms are the same in both singular and plural. (There is an old second person singular form which is found in the literature of the past and sometimes in modern church services: *thou art, thou dost, thou hast*, etc.)

Third Person: a verb is in the third person singular if the subject is any other singular word, and in the third person plural if the subject is any other plural word.

These categories have little importance and need not be memorised. What is important to remember, however, is that *the nature of the subject affects the form of the verb*. Some problems associated with this rule are dealt with in the next section.

8 Some points about subjects

(*a*) Sometimes two or three singular nouns are linked together to form a subject which thus becomes plural:

>The ship *is leaving* the harbour.

but

>The ship and its tug *are leaving* the harbour.

This may seem a very simple rule, but it is surprising how often, especially in a long sentence when the subject and the verb are separated by several other words or groups of words, a sentence which has a singular subject acquires a plural verb, or vice versa.

A few plural nouns (*politics, news, mathematics*) take singular verbs, and so do a few expressions which are plural but which are so common that they are thought of as a single entity (*fish and chips, whisky and soda*, etc.) Thus

>How much *is* gin and tonic?
>*Is* there any salt and pepper?

(*b*) *There is* must be used if the complement is singular, and *there are* if the complement is plural:

>There is *no good reason* for refusing.
>There are *pen and paper* on the sideboard.

(*c*) Collective nouns (see Chapter 2, section 2(*b*)) may take either a singular or a plural verb. To be quite precise, use a singular verb if the sense of the sentence stresses the entity of the collective noun, and a plural verb is the sense stresses the diversity of the collection:

>The crew *was* well trained.
>The crew *were* made up of English, French, Indians and Lascars.

In the first sentence the crew is regarded as a single unit, so the verb appears in the singular. In the second sentence, the crew are regarded as a number of individuals, so the plural is used.

If it is decided to put a sentence into the singular, the sentence should not then be allowed to stray into the plural, or vice versa, as has happened in the following:

The nation *was* facing *their* worst ordeal.

The council *are* giving the matter *its* immediate attention.

The Board of Directors *is* convinced that *they* have a good chance of success in launching the new product.

(*d*) The following words are singular: *everybody*, *everything*, *everyone*, *somebody*, *each one*, *each*, *nobody*, *no-one*. The expressions *each of* (*the*), *either of* (*the*), *neither of* (*them*) must also have singular verbs:

Each of us *has* three votes.

but

Both of us *have* three votes.

(*e*) *Either . . . or* and *neither . . . nor* must be followed by a singular verb, provided that the alternative nouns which follow each part of the expression are singular:

Neither his brother nor his sister *was* able to help.

If one of the halves of the expression is plural (or if both halves are), the verb must be in the plural:

Neither his brothers nor his sister *were* able to help.

Exercise 55

Supply the correct form of the verb.

1. Bacon and eggs (is, are) on the menu.
2. 'Pickwick Papers' (was, were) written by Dickens.
3. Physics (were, was) the subject in which he was specialising.
4. The scissors (is, are) blunt.
5. Either the manufacturer or the shop-keeper (is, are) responsible.
6. Everyone from the surrounding villages (were, was) there.
7. The team (were, was) drawn from England, Scotland, Wales and Ireland.

8. The news at last (give, gives) grounds for hope.
9. Neither the driver nor his passenger (remember, remembers) what happened.
10. The school (were, was) assembled by nine o'clock.
11. There (is, are) no differences of opinion.
12. The committee (was, were) undecided.
13. Each of the boys (were, was) hoping to be selected.
14. Neither of the alternatives (are, is) very attractive.
15. Somebody in one of the bedrooms (were, was) playing the gramophone very loudly.
16. The jury (is, are) expected to return their verdict later today.
17. If either of them (phone, phones), please take a message.
18. Neither my colleagues nor I (am, are) going on holiday at Easter.

9 Tense

Consider the following sentences:

> He walks with a limp.
> He walked with a limp.
> He will walk with a limp.

In the first sentence, the verb expresses an action going on in present time. The verb is said to be *in the present tense*. In the second sentence, the verb expresses an action going on in the past: the verb in this sentence is said to be *in the past tense*. In the third sentence, the verb expresses an action that will happen in time to come: this verb is said to be *in the future tense*.

The general reader needs to know only that verbs have three tenses, past, present and future. The following details of these tenses need not be memorised.

(a) *Present tenses*
Compare the following:

> He walks with a limp.
> He is walking with a limp.

Both of these are present tenses, but the emphasis in the second sentence is on the fact that the action of the verb is continuing. The form of the verb in the second sentence is called the *present continuous*, to distinguish it from the *simple present* of the first sentence. Another difference between the two tenses is that the simple present denotes a habitual action, and the continuous present an action that is happening now, but not necessarily habitually.

My dog runs very fast.

means that the dog habitually runs very quickly: the sentence does not necessarily imply that the dog is actually running at the time the sentence was spoken or written.

My dog is running very quickly.

implies that the action of running is taking place at the time the sentence is spoken or written.

The present tense in English is a very flexible one:

The shops are open on Sundays.

means that the shops are habitually open on Sundays, and will therefore be open next Sunday, in the future. The sentence does not necessarily mean that the shops are actually open at the time the sentence is uttered.

The sun rises at eight minutes past six tomorrow.

means *the sun will rise*: this is an example of the way in which the present tense can, by common usage, refer to the future.

The present tense is sometimes used to describe past events in a way which make them more immediate, vivid and alive. Here is part of a description of a battle which took place in 1916, and which was written about many years later:

At Delville, infantry of the 24th Division slowly force back the German line. A day later, a brave Irish attack results in the capture of Ginchy, and pursues the Germans through the village. Three kilted pipers stop to play among the ruins.

The present tense does not imply that these events are happening now, or that they were actually happening at the time the author was writing about them. The present tense is simply a literary device, making a change from the past tense in which history is normally described.

Exercise 56

In which of the following sentences is the verb in the present tense?

1. It was raining when we arrived.   2. They scoured the hills without success.   3. Is there any truth in the story?   4. Which theatre are you going to this evening?   5. We start work to-morrow.   6. Butter prices rose.   7. He has a silk scarf round his neck.   8. Will you be at home today?   9. The prospects look good.   10. He had now run out of patience.

(b) *Past tenses*
In the sentence
He *visited* Cheddar Gorge.
the action of the verb is in the past. This is an example of the *simple past* tense.
He *was visiting* Cheddar Gorge.
is another example of the continuous tense, with the emphasis on the fact that the action was continuing. The tense is called the *past continuous*.

He was visiting Cheddar Gorge when he met his future
    wife.
is an example of the two tenses in the same sentence. The continuous tense *was visiting* implies that the visit was spread over a period of time in the past, during which time the single action of meeting his future wife – a shorter action than *visiting* – took place, also in the past. This action is therefore expressed in the simple past tense *met*.
He *had visited* Cheddar Gorge.
stresses that the action of visiting was complete. This tense (with *had*) is called the *pluperfect* (or *past perfect*). Its use is often to state that one action was completed as another began

After he *had visited* Cheddar Gorge he decided to visit
    Bath.
The train *had travelled* nearly a hundred miles before the
    fire was detected.
When the guests *had finished* their meal, the concert began.
Another tense is the *perfect tense* (which some refer to as the

present perfect and regard as a present tense, though this is probably confusing for the general reader):

He *has visited* the Cheddar Gorge.

The emphasis here is that the action is completed in the present, i.e. at the time of writing or speaking. The difference between

We *decided* not to go. (simple past)

and

We *have decided* not to go. (perfect)

is that the latter action of deciding has occurred nearer the present time than the former one.

Exercise 57

In which of the following sentences is there a verb in the past tense?

1. There was a pause. 2. They had not seen each other for several months. 3. What did he want? 4. They were confused. 5. Are they engaged yet? 6. As she grew up, she went less often. 7. He was walking past his brother's warehouse. 8. I had not intended to begin today. 9. The children burst into the room. 10. Last year's holiday remains in the memory.

(c) Future tense

To express the future, *shall* is used with the first persons singular and plural (i.e. *I* and *we*), and *will* with all other words. It is incorrect, though increasingly common, to say *I will, we will* to express the future tense. (For further comments on *will* and *shall*, see section 14(c).)

There are few forms of the future tense.

I *shall reply* to your letter this evening.

The train *will leave* from platform five.

These are examples of the straightforward future tense, or *simple future*: they are statements of what will happen in time to come. They are very little different from the *future continuous*:

I *shall be replying* to your letter this evening.

The train *will be leaving* from platform five.

though this continuous tense, as with the present and past

continuous tenses, places some emphasis on the length of time the action will take.

I *shall have replied* to your letter this evening.

means at some time in the future (i.e. this evening), the action of the verb (i.e. replying) will have been completed. This is an illustration of the *future perfect* tense, which denotes an action that will have been completed by some point of time in the future.

The tense which is called *the future in the past* sounds to be a contradiction in terms, but it indicates an action which, at some time in the past, was then rightly regarded as future. Compare

(i) 'I shall travel overnight,' the detective decided.
(ii) The detective decided that he would travel overnight.

In the first sentence we learn that, at some time in the past (*decided*), the detective made plans for the future (*shall travel*). The second sentence merely says the same thing in a different way, and *would travel* is an example of the *future in the past*. The *future continuous* and the *future perfect* can also appear in this form:

He decided that he *would be travelling* overnight (continuous).

He calculated that he *would have been travelling* for six hours by the time he reached his destination (future perfect).

Exercise 58

In which of these sentences is there a verb in one of the future tenses?

1. They will find it difficult.   2. He has reasons for all his actions.   3. We must send him a birthday-card next month. 4. I shall have finished before long.   5. I shall see what I can find.

(*d*)   *Summary of tenses*:

What has been said so far about tenses can be put in another way:

Simple tenses:

Present	I write, he writes
Past	I wrote, he wrote
Future	I shall write, he will write
Future in the Past	I should write, he would write

Continuous Tenses:

Present	I am writing, he is writing
Past	I was writing, they were writing
Future	I shall be writing, he will be writing
Future in the Past	I should be writing, he would be writing

Perfect Tenses:

Present	I have written, he has written
Past	I had written, he had written
Future	I shall have written, he will have written
Future in the Past	I should have written, he would have written

For everyday purposes, however, it is seldom necessary to go beyond the terms *past*, *present* and *future*.

Exercise 59

Write out the above tables, putting in the forms for *we* and *they* instead of *I* and *he*. Before doing so, look up the rule for *shall* and *will*, and apply it to *should* and *would*.

Exercise 60

State the tense of the verbs in the following passage.

The traveller had been boasting all evening of his exploits when he had hunted wild animals in Africa.

'I am telling you what I have actually seen for myself,' he declared. 'After a few weeks' rest I shall return to the jungle, as I long for more adventures.'

The barman asked him if he had ever visited Egypt.

'Egypt?' said the traveller. 'I visited Egypt six years ago. I shall be staying in Cairo for a few weeks on my way to the jungle. How well I remember that visit to Egypt!'

'What happened?' asked the barman.

'I'll tell you,' answered the traveller, who beamed at the prospect of another story. 'I had gone to Egypt at the suggestion of a friend who had promised me a visit to some excavations he was making. Well, I made some wonderful discoveries. One was specially notable. I found the skeleton of Moses in the bullrushes.'

The barman burst out into laughter.

'What are you laughing at?' said the traveller. 'I'm telling you the truth.'

10   Active and passive

Consider the following sentences:

The secretary typed the letter.

The letter was typed by the secretary.

Although there is the same meaning in each sentence, there is a slight difference of emphasis. In the first sentence, the attention is specially drawn to *the secretary*, which is the subject of the sentence. In the second sentence, the emphasis is placed on the letter, which is the subject of the sentence.

When the subject of a verb performs the action described in the verb, the verb is said to be *active* (or *in the active voice*). The first of the two sentences quoted above has a verb which is active.

When the subject of a verb receives or suffers the action of the verb, the verb is said to be passive (or *in the passive voice*). The second sentence has a passive verb, because the subject (*the letter*) undergoes the action (*was typed*) denoted by the verb.

Sometimes the passive voice is used because the subject of the verb in the active voice would be unknown:

He *was condemned* to seven years imprisonment.

We do not know – and it apparently does not matter – who did the condemning.

It is a useful rule, when writing English, to use the active voice in preference to the passive whenever possible. The effect is stronger and more direct, and fewer words are normally used – which is usually a good point of style.

It may be noted that some nouns have an active and a passive sense, e.g. *employer* (one who employs) and *employee* (one who is employed); *creator* (one who creates) and *creation* (that which is created); *examiner* and *examinee*.

Exercise 61

Pick out the verbs in the passive voice, and state their subjects.

1. The local residents were angered by the proposals. 2. They will be opposed tooth and nail. 3. Have you been told about the plan? 4. The shop-keepers are being canvassed for their opinion. 5. I can suffer this inconvenience no longer. 6. You have been warned. 7. They will be sailing on Wednesday. 8. The speech was favourably received. 9. Millions of gallons are shipped abroad annually. 10. He received the news calmly.

Exercise 62

Rewrite the following in the passive voice.

1. The moon lights up the scene.
2. My neighbour will probably take it.
3. The storm may well destroy the harvest.
4. My wife wrote the letter.
5. We all took a rest under the shade of a boulder.
6. All the candidates should carefully study the instructions.
7. That will teach him a lesson.
8. A farmer showed us a short cut.

Exercise 63

Rewrite the following in the active voice.

1. The ship was sunk by a mine.
2. This work can easily be done by small children.
3. The choruses were sung by all four choirs.
4. Road works were begun by council workmen.
5. Not a word was spoken by any of the prisoners.

6. The toast was drunk by all present.
7. The Channel was swum by fifteen people last year.
8. He was forsaken by all his friends.
9. A surprise was sprung on him by his colleagues.
10. It was hidden by the cat.

Exercise 64

Each of the following contains an error in the form of the passive voice. What is it?

1. The congregation was bade to be seated. 2. An interesting play was broadcasted last evening. 3. Such a burden of taxation cannot be born indefinitely. 4. The car was broke up. 5. The motor-bike has been rode too hard. 6. Half of the sandwiches have been ate. 7. The carpet has been badly lain. 8. Dirt has been trod over the floor.

11 Mood

A verb may denote an action or state of being in one of four ways which are called *moods*. The mood is the form which shows the manner in which the action of the verb is represented.

(*a*) When a verb states a fact or asks a question, it is said to be in the *Indicative Mood*, or more simply, it is said to be *indicative*:
> Nobody *loves* me.
> *Does* nobody *love* me?
This mood occurs more frequently than any other.

(*b*) When a verb expresses a command, it is said to be in the *Imperative Mood* or, more simply, *in the imperative*:
> *Pass* the pepper, please.
> Right *turn*!
Verbs in the imperative have no stated subject, but it is 'understood' to be an unspecified 'you':
> (Will you) *pass* the pepper, please.
> (You must now) *turn* right.

(*c*) A verb may make a statement in a general way, without any reference to a person or a thing:

To chop down the trees was unforgivable.

This sentence refers to the act of chopping without stating who or what performed the act, i.e. the verb has no subject. This form of verb is called the *infinitive* (see also section 13), and can normally be recognised because the word *to* precedes it. The infinitive is used as the equivalent of a noun in that it can act as the subject of a sentence

To err is human.

or as the object

He wants *to travel*

The infinitive can be in the present or the past tense. Examples of the present infinitive are *to find*, *to give*, *to be*, *to steal*, *to run*. Examples of the past infinitive (sometimes called the perfect infinitive) are *to have found*, *to have given*, *to have been*, *to have stolen*, *to have run*. Here are examples of sentences containing present and past infinitives:

It is more blessed *to give* than *to receive*.

To have attempted a rescue in such weather would have been folly.

The infinitive also occurs in the active and the passive. The above present infinitives become, in the passive, *to be found*, *to be given*, *to be*, *to be stolen*, *to be run*. The above past infinitives become, in the passive, *to have been found*, *to have been given*, *to have been*, *to have been stolen*, *to have been run*.

There are many other forms of the infinitive, for example in the continuous tense (*to be finding*, *to have been giving*, etc.), but it is sufficient to be able to recognise an infinitive; detailed classification is irrelevant.

There is no form for the future infinitive, which is expressed by using *about* followed by the present infinitive:

He is about to leave.

There are occasions when the infinitive is not preceded by *to*, especially when the infinitive comes after a verb such as *make*, *see*, *can*, *must*, etc.:

The shock made him (to) tremble.

Crowds saw her (to) arrive.

Millions heard him (to) sing.

Note that the past infinitive is often used in speech or writing when the present infinitive is in fact sufficient:

I should have liked to have been there.

has two past tenses (*should have liked*, and the past infinitive *to have been*): one would have been sufficient:

I should have liked to be there.

or

I should like to have been there.

(*d*)   A verb may be found in a particular form if it states a condition, a purpose, a wish or a doubt. This form is called the *subjunctive mood*. The subjunctive is often indistinguishable from the indicative in form, but it can be seen as a separate form in the following types of sentences:

  (i) expressing certain forms of a wish:

Long *live* the Queen!

 (ii) expressing an unfulfilled wish:

Would I *had had* more time.

This form is now dated.

(iii) after *if*, expressing a condition, when the words after *if* are not fact:

If they *were* less ruthless, they would be more popular.
I shouldn't do it, if I *were* you.

If, however, the words after *if* contain a condition which might be fulfilled, the straightforward indicative is used:

If it *rains*, the concert *will be held* indoors.

The subjunctive is only found when the condition after *if* cannot, or is very unlikely to, be fulfilled. Even so, nowadays, it would not be regarded as incorrect to use the indicative forms (*he was, I was*) in such sentences.

(iv) after *lest*:

Take care lest the garage *charge* you more than it should.

 (v) after *as if* and *as though*, when the words following them are not accepted as true:

He referred to his wife as if *she were* an idiot.

(vi) after *that*, expressing a purpose or wish:

> I wish that *I were* a thousand miles away.
> He proposed that the plan *be* shelved.

It will be seen from the above examples that the main forms of the subjunctive are as follows:

(*a*) the third person singular of the present tense of the subjunctive is the same as the plural form of the indicative. The verb *live* in *Long live the Queen* is the third person singular of the present tense of the subjunctive, and *live* is the form found in the plural form of the indicative (*they live*). In the sentence quoted as illustration in (iv) above, *the garage charge* is the subjunctive: the indicative would have been *charges*, but *charge* is the subjunctive form, identical with the plural (*the charge*).

(*b*) *were* is used with the first and third person singular (*I were, he were, she were, it were*), instead of the indicative *was*. Otherwise the subjunctive is indistinguishable from the indicative when *were* is used in other persons.

(*c*) *be* is used throughout the present tense of *to be*, as in (vi) above.
The indicative form is *I am, you are, he/she/it is, we are, they are.*
The subjunctive forms, rather dated, are *I be, you be, he be*, etc.

Exercise 65

In which of the four moods are the verbs in the following.

1. So be it. 2. What did he say? 3. She was afraid to enter.
4. If need be, we can arrange to be telephoned. 5. Please sit down. 6. If the manager were here he would be able to answer your question. 7. He requested that I be kept informed. 8. Did you see them leave? 9. Be careful lest he fall. 10. He spoke as though it were a matter of no importance.

12 Finite and non-finite

In the sentence
> She fled into the kitchen.

the verb *fled* is in which tense? Singular or plural? First, second or third person? The verb *fled* has a tense, number (singular or plural) and person. It is *limited* to its tense, number and person. A verb thus limited is said to be *finite*. A finite verb always has a subject.

Man is sometimes spoken of as finite because he is limited in his function. But we refer to space as infinite because it is limitless. Now consider:

(i) Seeing the monkey, I joined the crowd of spectators.
(ii) Seeing the monkey, you joined the crowd of spectators.
(iii) Seeing the monkey, we joined the crowd of spectators.
(iv) Seeing the monkey, the visitors joined the crowd of spectators.

Seeing is formed from the verb *see*, and is therefore part of a verb.

In (i) *seeing* refers to *I* (first person singular)
  (ii) *seeing* refers to *you* (second person, singular or plural)
  (iii) *seeing* refers to *we* (first person plural)
  (iv) *seeing* refers to *the visitors* (third person plural)

In other words, the form *seeing* can be used in all four instances. Whether it refers to first, second or third person, singular or plural, it remains the same. It is not a finite verb, with a subject: we can say *I see, we saw, they will see, we will be seeing*, but not *I seeing, you seeing, he seeing*, etc. In the sentences quoted, *seeing* is not limited to person and number (singular or plural): it is a *non-finite* (or *infinite*) part of the verb. A non-finite verb has no subject.

  Similarly in
  Worn out by their long walk, the children soon fell asleep.
the word *worn* is formed from the verb *to wear*: it is a *part* of the verb. *Worn* remains the same if the children it describes fall asleep in different circumstances:

  Worn out by their long walk, the children soon *fall* asleep.
  Worn out by their long walk, the children *will* soon *fall* asleep.

In other words, *worn* is a verb-form which is not affected by changes in tense. *Fell, fall, will fall* change their form to denote tense: they are finite verbs with the subject being *the children*. *Worn*, in the above sentences, is a non-finite verb, not limited to past, present or future tense. It has no subject: one can say *they wear*, *they were worn*, *they have been worn*, *they will be worn*, etc., but not *I worn*, *they worn*, etc.

Exercise 66

State whether the verbs italicised in the following are finite or non-finite.

1. *Picking* his way up the rough track, he *made* for the barn.   2. *Seizing* his opportunity, he *rushed* out.   3. *Admired* by many, he *was loved* by none.   4. She *was holding* the baby when the phone rang.   5. *Having discovered* the error, the firm *did* their best *to correct* it.

13 Non-finite verbs

Non-finite verbs are those parts of verbs which have no subjects. There are three kinds of non-finite verb: the infinitive, the participle and the gerund.

(a) *The infinitive* has already been discussed above (section 11(c)). It is sufficient to repeat briefly that the infinitive is, as its name indicates, a non-finite part of the verb because it has no subject. It merely names the verb:

> He expects *to succeed*.
> *To have failed* was unthinkable

In these two sentences, the infinitive has the same function as a noun; in the first sentence the present infinitive *to succeed* is the object of the verb *expects*; in the second sentence the past infinitive *to have failed* is the subject of *was*. In fact both infinitives could be replaced by nouns:

> He expects *success*.
> *Failure* was unthinkable.

The unity of the infinitive is often broken by the insertion of another word, e.g. to *finally* succeed; to *previously* fail; to *fondly* hope. These are examples of what is called the *split infinitive*. It used to be said that a split infinitive was always an error of grammar. There are occasions, however, when an attempt to avoid a split infinitive produces clumsiness or even ambiguity. The best rule is to avoid splitting the infinitive if possible, but to use a split infinitive if it gives a smoother reading and avoids ambiguity. Such occasions will be rare.

Note that *to have previously failed* is not a split infinitive: *to previously have failed* is. The infinitive is split only if a word is introduced between *to* and the word which forms the infinitive with it: in the example quoted, the infinitive is *to have*, and *failed* is a past participle, a term to be explained shortly. In other words, an infinitive is split only if the splitting word comes immediately after the *to*.

(*b*)   *The participle.* In section 12, it was explained that in

Seeing the monkey, the visitors joined the crowd of spectators.

seeing is a non-finite part of the verb *see* because it has no subject. It is an example of what is called the *present participle*. The present participle always ends in *-ing* (but not all words ending in *-ing* are present participles). In the example quoted, *seeing* is doing the work of an adjective by describing the noun *visitors*.

Also in section 12 it was explained that in

Worn out by their long walk, the children soon fell asleep.

worn is a non-finite part of the verb *wear*. It has no subject. It too is a participle, a *past participle*, doing the work of an adjective in describing *the children*. The past participle normally ends in *-en*, *-ed*, *-d* or *t*.

The participle may be separated from the noun it describes, as in the two sentences quoted, where *seeing* is separated from *the visitors*, and *worn* is separated from *the children*. Or the participle may be placed next to the noun, exactly like an adjective:

blinding rain, a *howling* wind, the *advancing* army   (present participles)

broken crockery, a *torn* jacket, the *cut* finger (past participles)

It will now be recognised that participles are used when forming tenses of verbs (they had *written*, to have *failed*, are you *coming*) and when forming the active and passive (he was *carrying*, he was *carried*).

Exercise 67

Supply suitable present participles for the following nouns (e.g. rock – *falling*):

game, book, character, flower, clothes, snow, darkness, sun.

Exercise 68

Supply suitable past participles for the following nouns (e.g. rock – *fallen*):

toy, room, present, building, grass, goods, liquid, wood.

Exercise 69

What is the past participle of the following verbs?

steer, carry, commit, wear, do, win, write, be, have, weave, benefit, drive, begin, dig, eat, find, hold, shoot, freeze, strike, speak, sell, tear, read, creep, mean, think, buy, leave, bite.

Exercise 70

Pick out the participles in the following, and say what words they describe.

1. He was a member of the winning team.
2. Fallen leaves lay everywhere.
3. Being a methodical man, he still had the receipt.
4. She sat down, overcome with joy.
5. The painting is again on show, having now been restored.
6. The painting, having now been restored, is again on show.
7. Having now been restored, the painting is again on show.
8. The police restored order.

9. The photographs have been lost.
10. Having beaten the eggs, mix them with the cream.

(*c*) *The participle*, being an adjective, must be clearly related to a noun or a noun-equivalent. Examine this sentence:

Being windy, we could not keep our umbrellas open.

To what word in the sentence does *being windy* refer? There is no word to which it belongs. The participle is unrelated. The sentence can be corrected in one of two ways:

(i) by supplying a word for the participle to relate to.

The weather being windy, we could not keep our umbrellas open.

This is now clear and correct. (The words *The weather being windy* are what is called an Absolute Construction because the construction has a subject (nominative) and the whole phrase is *absolute* or separate from the construction of the rest of the sentence.) Alternatively:

Being windy, the weather prevented us from keeping our umbrellas open.

the rule is that a participle must have a noun or noun equivalent to relate to, and that the participle should be as close as possible to its noun. See the following exercise for typical errors in this respect.

(ii) By turning the participle into a finite verb so that it is quite clear what the verb relates to.

As the weather (or it) was windy, we could not keep our umbrellas open.

Exercise 71

Correct the following examples of unrelated participles.

1. Arriving late, all the best seats had already been sold.
2. Being Wednesday afternoon, the shops were shut.
3. Standing on the platform, a trolley ran over my foot.
4. Banging the door, there was a complaint from upstairs.
5. Hoping to reduce his temperature, a new drug was prescribed.

6. Regarded as a future Cabinet Minister, his losing the election was a severe blow to his party.
7. Being wet, I decided not to go.
8. Arising out of the collision, a man appeared in court.
9. While not wishing to contradict, my opinion is that the difficulty could have been avoided.
10. After travelling all day, a good night's rest is what they will need.

(d) *The gerund* is a verbal noun, i.e. it is a part of the verb, but its function in a sentence is similar to that of a noun:

> *Walking* is healthy exercise.
> He enjoys *cycling*.

These two gerunds are formed from the verbs *to walk* and *to cycle*. The first is the subject of the sentence: the second is the object.

A gerund itself can take an object.

> Painting *the ceiling* will be difficult.
> Finding *a hotel* took a long time.

It will be noted that the gerund is like the present participle in ending in *-ing*, but there need be no confusion provided that the function of the *-ing* word is thought out:

> The *complaining* passengers were offered a refund.
> He was led away *complaining*.
> *Complaining* is not likely to get us anywhere.
> *Complaining* about the weather is futile.

In the first sentence, *complaining* describes *passengers*, a noun; *complaining* is doing the work of an adjective and is therefore a participle. In the second sentence, *complaining* describes *He*, and is again adjectival. In the third sentence, *Complaining* is the subject of the sentence, and subject of the verb *is*; it is therefore doing the work of a noun, and is a gerund. The same is true of the fourth sentence, despite the separation of *Complaining* and *is*.

Exercise 72

Pick out the gerunds in the following.

1. Striking miners lobbied MPs yesterday.   2. They claim that

striking is the only course of action open to them.   3. Hitting a dog is not the way to train it.   4. It is foolish to mix drinking and driving.   5. The water is unfit for drinking.   6. Drinking tea is a national pastime.   7. Drinking water is in short supply. 8. Having arrived at the airport, they found that all planes were grounded.

(*e*) *The gerund* sometimes gives rise to mistakes of grammar. Consider

He doesn't like his daughter staying up late.

What is the object of *doesn't like*? Not *his daughter*, presumably, but her *staying up late*. In fact, *staying* is a gerund, a noun equivalent, and *daughter* should be in the possessive (see Chapter 2 section 5) because she '*owns*' the *staying up late.*
Thus

He doesn't like his *daughter's* staying up late.

Just as one would say

His early arrival was a surprise.

one should say

His arriving early was a surprise.

where *arriving* is a noun equivalent (i.e. a gerund replacing the noun *arrival*) needing the possessive *his*. Yet most people would say

They were surprised at *him* arriving early.

even though the grammatical function of *arriving* is identical, i.e. it is a gerund, which could be exchanged for a noun:

They were surprised at *his* early arrival.

The error is so common that it probably occurs more often than the correct form. Other examples of wrong use:

They objected to *him* playing the trumpet in the middle of
    the night.

They are inconvenienced by their *car* having broken down.

The words needed are *his* and *car's*, possessive forms to go with the gerunds.

14 Sentence, clause and phrase

Now that the verb has been discussed fairly thoroughly, it is possible to set out certain important definitions, even though some of them are not yet complete.

A *sentence* is a group of words which makes complete sense and contains a finite verb:

> He has an uncontrollable temper.

A *clause* is a group of words which includes a finite verb and forms part of a sentence. Without it a sentence may not make complete sense:

> He has a temper *that cannot be controlled.*

The finite verb in the clause, *cannot*, has the subject *that*. The clause is doing the work done by the adjective *uncontrollable* in the first sentence. It is an *adjectival clause*. A fuller definition of *clause* is found in Chapter 12.

A *phrase* is a group of words without a finite verb:

> *Having an uncontrollable temper*, he is unpopular.

Here, the phrase contains the non–finite verb *having*, which is a present participle describing *he*. Because the phrase is doing the work of an adjective, it is called an *adjectival phrase*.

> *Having an uncontrollable temper* makes him unpopular.

is a sentence: it makes complete sense and contains a finite verb *makes*, of which the subject is the italicised phrase. The phrase is therefore doing the work of a noun; *having* is a gerund, a verbal noun. In this sentence, the phrase is called a *noun phrase*.

This subject is dealt with at greater length in Chapter 12.

Exercise 73

Complete the following with suitable adjectival clauses:

1. She was carrying a suitcase which . . . .
2. The boy made a boat which . . . .
3. I was offered a book that . . . .
4. The manager, who . . . , decided to retire.
5. The man whom . . . has worked very well.

Exercise 74

Identify the adjectival clauses and suggest a single adjective which conveys the same meaning.

1. He made a remark which could be interpreted in two ways.
2. She wore an outfit which was not suitable for the occasion.
3. This is an act of folly for which there can be no excuse.
4. It was a consequence from which there was no escape.
5. He is a man who is always in a good humour.
6. It is the town where I was born.

15   Miscellaneous

(*a*)   In many instances a word may be used as a verb in one context and as a noun or some other part of speech in another context. Just as people can have different functions – a man can be an *engineer* at work, a *gardener* at home, and the *secretary* of a local committee – so can words: a cricketer may *run* (verb) or make *a run* (noun).

Exercise 75

Construct sentences using the following words as (i) nouns, (ii) verbs:

part, guard, blow, work, dream, sweep, round, book, help, close.

(*b*)   A difference in function may be indicated by a difference in pronunciation, even though a word's spelling may be unchanged. For example, one of the words in the previous exercise, *close*, rhymes with *rose* when it is a verb (please *close* the door) and with *dose* when it is an adjective (a *close* shave) or a noun (a cathedral's *close*). The word *conduct* is pronounced with the stress on *con-* when the word is a noun meaning *behaviour*, and with the stress on *-duct* when it is a verb meaning *guide*.

Exercise 76

What difference of pronunciation is used in the following words to indicate difference in function as nouns and verbs?

1. convert   2. convict   3. contest   4. lead   5. combine
6. escort   7. transfer   8. present.

(c)   It was explained in section 9 (c) that *shall* is used with the first person (*I, we*) to express the future, and that *will* is used in all other cases to express the future. These two words have other important uses, however. It is common to use *will* in the first person to express willingness, determination, obligation or permission, and *shall* in all other cases. In other words, the rule for forming the future tense is the opposite of that for expressing willingness, etc. Thus

  I (or *we*) shall be surprised if he comes.   (expressions of
    futurity)
  I (or *we*) will write tomorrow.   (expression of determination or willingness)

but

  The plane will refuel at Athens.   (expression of futurity)
  They shall not pass.   (expression of determination)

These rules are often ignored, *shall* and *will* being used interchangeably, but it is still good English to use *shall* with *I* and *we* to express the plain future.

Exercise 77

Say what is the function of *shall* and *will* in the following:

1. I shall be forty next birthday.   2. He shall never be invited again.   3. We shall be there before nightfall.   4. I'll go.   5. The rates will go up next year.   6. I won't take no for an answer.
7. I shan't know before next weekend.   8. Members shall pay their subscriptions annually.

(d)   Some people find difficulty in distinguishing between the verbs *to lie* and *to lay*.

The verb *to lie* means (i) to speak falsely (ii) to be at rest. It is intransitive. The past tense is *lay* and the past participle *lain*:

> He lies.   (present tense)
> He is lying low.   (present continuous)
> He lay on the grass.   (past tense)
> It has (*or* had) lain idle for months.

The verb *to lay* means to place, deposit, impose, dispose, etc. It is transitive. The past tense is *laid*; so is the past participle:

> They lay their hopes on a fine summer.   (present tense)
> They are laying a new underground cable.   (present continuous)
> She laid the table.   (past tense)
> All was laid bare.

Exercise 78

Write down, as fully as you can, the answers to the following questions, then refer to earlier parts of the chapter to check the accuracy of what you have written:

1. What is a verb?
2. How do you find the subject of a verb?
3. How do you find the object of a verb?
4. What is the difference between transitive and intransitive verbs?
5. What is a complement?
6. What are the rules for using *shall* and *will*?
7. What is meant by describing verbs as active and passive?
8. What is meant by *imperative*?
9. What is an infinitive?
10. What is the difference between a finite and non-finite verb?
11. What is the difference between a participle and a gerund?
12. What is the difference between a clause and a phrase?

Exercise 79

Identify the finite verbs in the following, and state their subjects and objects:

The trumpet was duly sounded, the doors were thrown open, the attendant scampered for safety, and we all waited; but nothing happened at all. The attendant crept back and peered cautiously round the corner of the open doorway. He whistled and waved his cap. Gaining courage, he began to leap up and down in the mouth of the bull-pit, hooting and capering like a clown. Minutes passed, and still nothing happened. Slowly, at last, and sadly, lost as a young calf, the bull walked into the ring. He looked with bewilderment around him, turned back, found the doors shut, and began to graze in the sand. He had no conception of what was expected of him; all he wished was to be back in the brown pasture and to have no part of this. And when it came to the point, he put up no fight at all and was killed at last, without grace or honour, to the loud derision of the crowd.

(*Laurie Lee: adapted*)

Exercise 80

Identify all the passive verbs in the previous exercise.

Exercise 81

Pick out the infinitives in the following.

1. He likes to take a run and have a swim every morning. 2. It's not difficult to repair. 3. The door would not open. 4. Spectators can enter only by one entrance. 5. It would have been better to have travelled by train. 6. They are about to be married. 7. We could have helped if we had known. 8. I never heard him ring. 9. Can you make it work? 10. They must have forgotten to write.

Exercise 82

Which of the following contain participles and gerunds?

1. I was dimly aware of nights and days, of faces coming and going, of the grandmother sitting motionless, and of students peering in. 2. I remember waking in the dead of the night, to

hear the screech of a bird hovering over the silent town.   3. I felt doomed, resigned and full of infection.   4. I thought of the casual cuckoos and the climbing briars.   5. There followed days when sleeping and waking merged into each other.   6. Unmoved, I fell asleep, and woke to find the grandmother still seated by the bedside.   7. The low whispering of the students could still be heard.   8. I heard the stumbling of footsteps on the stairs.   9. From then on, I no longer heard the night-bird screeching over the town.   10. The trotting of donkeys, the tinkling of bells and the stirring of departing trains all suggested to me that the fever was over.

Exercise 83

Use the following in sentences (i) as transitive verbs (ii) as intransitive verbs:

mate, pour, heave, blow, turn.

Exercise 84

Use the following in sentences as (i) nouns (ii) verbs (iii) adjectives:

base, lay, wax, split, lead, shut, cut, set, light, mean.

Exercise 85

Write sentences using the following verbs as adjectives:

drop, swing, rush, stop, run, question.

5 The Adverb

1 Definition

If you think you may be late for your train, you walk *quickly* or *briskly* to the station: a burglar, on the other hand, may walk *stealthily* or *carefully* through the rooms of a house; someone carrying a heavy burden will walk *laboriously*, probably *slowly*; a drunk may walk *unsteadily*. All of the words *quickly, briskly, stealthily, carefully, laboriously, slowly, unsteadily* add to the meaning of the verb *walk*. They are called *adverbs*. An adverb tells us more about the action described in a verb, though this is not its sole function (see section 3 below). Most adverbs end in *-ly*.

The adverbs italicised in the previous paragraph add to the meaning of the verb *walk* by telling us *how* the action denoted by the verb (i.e. the action of walking) was done. They show the *manner* in which the action was performed, and are sometimes known as *adverbs of manner*. There are, of course, many other adverbs of manner that could apply to the verb *walk*. Someone who is busy may walk *purposefully*, someone who is lost may walk *aimlessly*, and so on.

An adverb of manner might be said to answer the question *How?* (e.g. How did he walk? He walked *furtively*.) Other types of adverb tell us different sorts of things about verbs. There are *adverbs of time*, which tell us *when* the action of verbs takes place (e.g. When did he arrive? He arrived *yesterday*), and *adverbs of place* which say *where* the action of verbs takes place (e.g. Where's the newspaper? It's *there*.) Further examples of adverbial functions are found in section 3 below.

Exercise 86

Supply adverbs of manner in the following.

1. He counted his money . . . .   2. The speaker apologised . . . for having arrived so late.   3. The guard dog barked . . . .   4. Did you sleep . . . ?   5. They were . . . rewarded.

Exercise 87

Supply six adverbs that could be used with each of the following verbs (e.g. speak *kindly*, *harshly*, *softly*, *vehemently*, *eloquently*, *persuasively*):

behave, write, dress, work, eat.

Exercise 88

In each of the following, replace the adverb with an alternative one.

1.   The suspect answered the questions well.
2.   The party is going well.
3.   The child reads nicely.
4.   The visitors behaved badly.
5.   The choir sang terribly.

Exercise 89

Supply suitable adverbs of time.

1.   I think the problem will . . . be solved.
2.   There are reports that the fighting is . . . at an end.
3.   The rebels have . . . surrendered.
4.   First we heard one story, and . . . we heard something quite different.
5.   But the news we have heard . . . sounds promising.

Exercise 90

Supply suitable adverbs of place:

1. . . . comes the bride.
2. Are you going . . . for your holidays this year?
3. The children have searched for it . . . .
4. Clouds of thick black smoke billowed . . . .
5. It's necessary to climb . . . to get the best view.

2 Adverb equivalents

(*a*) It is possible for a phrase to do the work of an adverb:

> You'll find it *behind the tea-pot*. (place)
> Handle it *with care*. (manner)
> Please reply *as soon as possible*. (time)

Such phrases are known as *adverbial phrases*.

(*b*) A clause may do the work of an adverb:

He behaved *as I expected him to*. (manner)
The ferry docked *as it was growing dark*. (time)

The reservoir has been built *where once there was an attractive valley*. (place)

Such clauses are known as *adverbial clauses* (of place, time and manner). Note that in all cases the clause adds to the meaning of a verb: *built* in the first sentence (telling *where* the reservoir had been built), *behave* in the second sentence (telling *how* he had behaved), and *docked* in the third (telling *when* the ferry had docked).

(*c*) The work of an adverb may be done by a word which is usually a noun or a verb (Let's go *home*. *Bang* goes another chance). To identify an adverb, always ensure that it is adding to the meaning of a verb. What matters is a word's function in a particular sentence, not its normal function.

Exercise 91

Expand the adverbs into adverbial phrases.

1. Their host acted *generously*.
2. We ought to set off *early*.
3. Does he still live *there*?
4. The party walked *quickly*.
5. Has he been *long* absent?

Exercise 92

Expand the adverbial phrases into clauses.

1. We shall go for a sail, *weather permitting*.
2. *With the approach of summer*, the days get longer.
3. They arrived *at nightfall*.
4. It's best to fish *in the deepest part of the river*.
5. We shall finish *before the end of the week*.

Exercise 93

Pick out the adverbs, adverbial phrases and adverbial clauses in the following. State whether they denote manner, place or time.

They stood solemnly outside the booking office. Each member of the party was dressed in black, and each held a wreath in his hand. The leader of the company then approached the ticket window. As he advanced, the rest followed him. Their clothes, their faces and their wreaths instantly betrayed their destination. Their speech equally betrayed their origin.

'Eight cheap returns to Perth,' said their leader in a gloomy voice, as he handed his wreath to his neighbour while he put his hand into his pocket.

'Eight?' asked the booking clerk as he peered through the window at the dour faces.

'Yes,' said the leader. 'We're all coming back later today.'

Exercise 94

The adverbs or adverbial equivalents in the following are clumsily placed. Rearrange the sentences.

1. All the guests who arrived quickly tucked in.
2. The last person to come promptly turned up at half past seven.
3. He should have given the voters more opportunities of seeing him in my view.
4. After we had had a swim with the help of a car-park attendant we managed to find somewhere to leave the car.

3 Other kinds of adverbs

(a) There are adverbs that denote the *degree* to which the action of a verb takes place: I *quite* like him; I like him *immensely*. Other common *adverbs of degree* include *too, much, more, most, so, completely, partly, utterly, mainly, rather, quite, fairly, very, exceedingly*.

Adverbs of degree may qualify adjectives and other adverbs:

It was an *exceptionally* hot afternoon. (describing the adjective *hot*)

He has worked *exceptionally* hard. (describing the adverb *hard*)

The definition of an adverb can now be fully stated: an adverb is a word that adds to the meaning of a verb, an adjective or another adverb.

Some adverbs of degree are over-worked in daily speech: *terribly* nice, *awfully* sorry, *fantastically* good. There is a danger that some of these, especially *awfully* and *terribly*, will lose their force and even their meaning because of unthinking over-use. Variety in vocabulary is to be recommended.

(b) There is a small group of adverbs called *interrogative adverbs*:

When are you taking up your new job?
Where did you find it?

How does it work?

Why don't you join us?

Interrogative adverbs always introduce questions, and indicate time (*When?*), place (*Where?*), manner (*How?*) or reason (*Why?*). Adverbial phrases might be used instead: in the above sentences the adverbs could be replaced by *on what date*, *in what place*, *in what way*, and *for what reason*.

(*c*) Finally, there is a small group of adverbs which does not fall into any of the above categories. It includes adverbs expressing affirmation (*certainly*, *surely*, *assuredly*) and doubt (*perhaps*, *probably*, *maybe*). The very common word *not* is an adverb, expressing the negation of a verb. The equally common words *yes* and *no* have sometimes been described as adverbs, but they are best regarded as sentence-equivalents, because they have the force of complete sentences and are merely convenient short-hand for complete sentences. If the answer to the question *Do you understand?* is *Yes*, the answer means *I do understand*; if *No*, the reply means *I do not understand*. This being so, *yes* and *no* act as sentences rather than adverbs.

Like all adverbs, the ones referred to in this section may be expanded into adverbial phrases:

certainly, surely	beyond a shadow of doubt, by all means
probably	in all probability
not	by no means

Exercise 95

Suggest alternatives for the following adverbs and adverbial equivalents:

1. He always looks *frightfully* smart.
2. That's *terribly* kind of you.
3. I'm *completely* at a loss to understand it.
4. It's *jolly* bad luck.
5. She's been *fantastically* lucky.

Exercise 96

Form adverbs from the following adjectives:

smooth, moody, dramatic, callous, majestic, gay, good, fast.

Exercise 97

Form adverbs from the following nouns:

moment, hour, day, sleep, length, heaven, side, shore.

Exercise 98

1. Can you think of any adjectives ending in -*ly* (e.g. stately)?
2. Can you form adverbs from them?
3. Can you think of any adjectives which cannot be turned into adverbs by adding -*ly*?

Exercise 99

Which of the italicised words are adjectives and which are adverbs?

1. The habitually *fast* driver is a menace.
2. The car took the corner extremely *fast*.
3. He telephoned *late* last night.
4. *Late* arrivals are not allowed into the theatre until a suitable moment.
5. Children find it hard to sit *still* for long.
6. The evening is very *still*.
7. It is *still* raining.
8. Milk is no longer delivered *daily*.
9. *Daily* delivery of newspapers is uncommon abroad.

4 Comparison of adverbs

Adverbs can be compared in the same way as adjectives (see Chapter 3, section 4):

Jack can run *fast*.
George can run *faster*.   (comparative)
Bob can run *fastest*.   (superlative)
She drives *carefully*.
Her daughter drives *more carefully*.   (comparative)
Her husband drives *most carefully*.   (superlative)

The comparative form is usually formed by using *more* before the adverb, and the superlative form by using *most*. Some short adverbs (such as *fast, hard, long*) form the comparative and superlative degrees by adding *-er* and *-est* respectively, just as many adjectives do.

Some degrees of comparison are irregular:

He normally works *well* but recently he has been working *better*, and as the exams approach I expect he will work *best* of all.

Also *little, less, least*; *much, more, most*.

Some adverbs have the same comparative and superlative forms as their corresponding adjectives:

adjective:	good	better	best
adverb:	well	better	best

adjective:	bad	worse	worst
adverb:	badly	worse	worst

The comparative form should be used when two people or things are being compared, and the superlative form when more than two are being compared:

Of the two candidates, he performed *better*.
Of the three candidates, he performed *best*.

The superlative form, however, is sometimes used not for the purposes of comparison but for emphasis:

Your application will be treated *most carefully*.

is not intended to imply that the 'treating' will be the most careful imaginable, or more careful than that given to other applications: the superlative merely stresses the high degree of carefulness being promised.

Exercise 100

Give the comparative degree of:

soon, tenderly, most, often, ill, further, fast.

5 Position of adverbs

Consider the following:

(i) Only the bridegroom hired a suit for the wedding.
(ii) The bridegroom only hired a suit for the wedding.
(iii) The bridegroom hired only a suit for the wedding.
(iv) The bridegroom hired a suit only for the wedding.

Only occupies a different position in each sentence. What difference of meaning is conveyed by the different position of *only*?

In the first sentence, the sense is that *only the bridegroom* (and no-one else) hired a suit. The second sentence means that he *only hired* (i.e. he did not buy, beg, borrow, steal, etc.) a suit. The third states that he hired *only a suit* (and nothing else, such as shoes or a shirt). The fourth means that he hired a suit *only for the wedding* (and not for the honeymoon or any other event).

Clearly, the placing of a word in a sentence can have considerable importance. The adverb should be placed as closely as possible to the word or group of words it qualifies, so as to avoid ambiguity or clumsiness. There is no objection to looseness in colloquial speech, where the tone of voice can help to suggest the intended meaning. Nor can there be any serious objection to such uses as *He only came yesterday*, which is perfectly clear, even though the perfectionist would prefer the more exact *He came only yesterday*. But there are occasions when the order of words is very significant, and the user of English would do well to cultivate precision and logic.

Exercise 101

Comment on the correctness of the following.

1. He merely plays the game for what he can get out of it.
2. The country will only remain a great world power as long as its people work hard.
3. I was rather impressed by his manner than by what he said.
4. He was shot at by his secretary, with whom he was finding fault, very fortunately without effect.
5. He only joined the club this year; now he thinks he's good enough to run it.

6   The nominative absolute

We have seen (in section 2(*b*)) that a clause can do the work of an adverb.   The following examples illustrate the full range of adverbial function that adverbial clauses can perform (these are dealt with more fully in Chapter 11):

The aircraft did not perform *as the designer intended.* (manner)

While it was being built, many changes were made.   (time)

Test flights took place *where there would be no inconvenience to other air-traffic.* (place)

Unless the weather was perfect, flights did not take place. (condition)

Although money was short, the project was completed. (concession)

There was a public outcry *because the plane was very noisy.* (cause)

The fuel-tanks were made large *so that refuelling stops would be unnecessary.* (purpose)

The aircraft became so heavy *that the number of passengers had to be restricted.* (result)

The final cost was bigger *than the Government had expected.* (comparison)

Sometimes, instead of an adverbial clause, a construction is used composed of a noun (or pronoun) together with a participle. Consider the following:

When the game was over, the spectators went home.

The game being over, the spectators went home.

The first of these contains an adverbial clause of time, stating *when* the action of *went home* took place. The second sentence contains a participial phrase instead of an adverbial clause: *being* is a participle (a verb without a subject), and the whole phrase does the work of the clause. This construction is called a *Nominative Absolute*, or simply an *Absolute Construction* (see Chapter 4, section 13(c)).

Revision

Exercise 102

For the adverbs in the following, substitute antonyms (i.e. words opposite in meaning). For instance: She walks *gracefully*; She walks *awkwardly*.

1. The interviewee answered *haltingly*.
2. He *willingly* agreed to a postponement.
3. He measured the glass *carefully*.
4. The sun has shone *continuously*.
5. Their car *often* breaks down.
6. He recounted his experiences *proudly*.

Exercies 103

Use the following groups of words in sentences (i) as adverbial equivalents, (ii) as adjectival equivalents, (iii) as noun equivalents. For example, *When the stranger arrived* could be used as follows:

(i) When the stranger arrived, the conversation ceased. (adverbial clause of time)

(ii) It happened on the day when the stranger arrived. (adjectival clause, describing *day*)

(iii) No-one could remember when the stranger arrived.   (noun
   clause, object of *remembered*)
1. when I retire   2. from here to Poland   3. where you live

Exercise 104

Write down definitions of the following, and then check the
accuracy of your answers by referring to the above chapter:

adverb; adverb of time; adverb of place; adverb of manner;
adverbial phrase; adverbial clause; adverb of degree; interrogative adverb; comparative degree of the adverb

Exercise 105

Say whether the italicised words are nouns, verbs, adjectives or
adverbs:

Everything *seemed* unreal and far off. Somebody brought him a
handful of moss *to press* against his shoulder, and he took it,
slipping his arm through the thong of his *spear*, and gathered
himself *slowly* upright. He looked about him at his fellows; and
the *familiar* faces looked *back*, silently, *not* quite *meeting* his eyes.

Exercise 106

Say whether the italicised phrases are noun phrases, adjectival
or adverbial phrases:

He could not speak *because of the dryness in his mouth*. *Pressing
the bandage to his wound*, he turned back in the direction that he
had come. Perhaps *drinking from the stream* would help. He could
still hear *shouting and the barking of dogs*, though they were now
receding *into the distance*. But there was a new pain *rolling over
him*. Would help never come?

Exercise 107

Say whether the italicised clauses are adjectival or adverbial
clauses, or neither:

He said *that he had been travelling for many years* in countries *which few men ever visited*. *Whenever he came home*, he brought many mementos from the places *which he had visited*. But *because he was now getting old*, he would retire from travelling *so that he could devote himself to writing*.

Exercise 108

Using a dictionary if necessary, give synonyms (words of the same meaning) and antonyms (words of opposite meaning) for the following:

1. *nouns*:   fear, health, greed, shame, departure.
2. *verbs*:   ask, defend, extend, trust, command.
3. *adjectives*:   ample, apt, talkative, urgent, discreet.
4. *adverbs*:   fast, sternly, well, carefully, firstly.

6   The Pronoun

1   Definition

We have seen that a noun is a word that names a person, place or
thing. It would, however, be very inconvenient if, whenever we
wanted to refer to a person, we had to give that person's name in
full. Whenever we refer to ourselves, for example, we use words
such as *I*, *me*, *my*, or *we*, *us*, *our*; if such words did not exist, we
should have to use our names in full; this would obviously be
rather long-winded and monotonous. Similarly, when we refer
to other people we use other short words such as *you*, *he*, *them*,
his, which are a sort of short-hand to avoid constantly using a
person's full name, or many people's full names; it may be necessary to use full names from time to time for identification, but
thereafter the shorter word is more convenient.

    Good morning, Mr Blake. How are *you*?

would have to be, if the useful little word *you* did not exist in the
language,

    Good morning, Mr Blake. How is Mr Blake?

and so on throughout the conversation. When referring to a
thing, we may say *it* or *its* instead of naming it by using a
noun.

    Instead of repeating nouns in full, then, we use words which
take the place of nouns. They are called pronouns, the *pro* part
meaning *instead of*. All the italicised words in the last paragraph
are pronouns. A pronoun refers to a person or thing without
actually naming it.

2 Personal pronouns

One person speaking of himself says *I* or *me*. Several persons speaking of themselves say *we* or *us*. These pronouns (italicised) are said to be *in the first person*. *I* and *me* are first person singular: *we* and *us* are first person plural.

A person addressing another person or a group of other persons says *you*. The pronoun *you* is said to be *in the second person*. The same word is used whether *you* is singular or plural.

A person speaking of another person will say *he* or *him* if the person is masculine, and *she* or *her* if the person is feminine. If one refers to a thing, one says *it*. These pronouns are said to be *in the third person*; all of them are singular. The third person plural forms are *they* or *them*, whether one is referring to masculine or to feminine persons, or to things.

All the pronouns italicised above are called *personal pronouns*.

3 Subject and object

A personal pronoun can be the subject of a sentence:

> *I* saw an owl.
> *You* must be joking.
> *He* is on holiday.

The pronouns are the subject because they are performing the action described in the verbs *saw*, *must* and *is*.

A personal pronoun can be the object of a sentence:

> The dog has swallowed *it*.
> I didn't recognise *you*.

The pronouns *it* and *you* are the objects of the verbs because they receive or 'suffer' the actions described in the verbs *swallowed* and *recognised*.

But note the following:

> (i) The boy kissed his mother.
> (ii) He kissed her.
> (iii) His mother hugged the boy.
> (iv) She hugged him.

In (i), *the boy* is the subject (of the verb *kissed*); in (iii), *the boy* is the object (of the verb *hugged*). The form of the words *the boy* is the same, whether subject or object. But now look at the two sentences (ii) and (iv). In (ii), the subject is *He* (a pronoun standing for *the boy*); in (iv), the object is *him* (also a pronoun standing for *the boy*). The form of the pronoun is different: it is *he* when acting as the subject (or *nominative*), and *him* when acting as the object (or *accusative*).

Similarly, *his mother* is the object (of *kissed*) in (i), and the subject (of *hugged*) in (iii). The corresponding pronoun is *her* in (ii) and *she* in (iv). Again, while the noun *mother* remains the same, whether subject or object, the pronoun has different forms.

Note also

> *I* saw *them*.   (*I* subject, *them* object)
> *They* saw *me*.   (*They* subject, *me* object)

The subject and object forms of personal pronouns may be summarised as follows:

	Subject (*i.e. nominative*)	*Object* (*i.e. accusative*)
First person singular	I	me
Second person singular and plural	you	you
Third person singular	he	him
	she	her
	it	it
First person plural	we	us
Third person plural	they	them

It will be noted that *you* and *it* are the same in the nominative and the accusative.

Pronouns are the only words in English that have different forms according to whether they are subject or object, though some nouns and verbs have different forms in the singular and the plural (*man has travelled far* but *men have travelled far*).

For an important rule about pronouns in the accusative, see the next chapter, section 2.

There is an old form of the second person singular pronoun which is *thou* (subject) and *thee* (object). This is found in the literature of former times (e.g. Shakespeare, and some translations of the Bible) and in devotional language, but otherwise it exists only in dialect speech in some parts of the country.

4   Some difficulties with pronouns

(*a*)   We have seen that there is an accusative form of the personal pronoun.
Study the sentence
> The telephone awoke my husband and me.

What is the verb in this sentence? What is its subject? What is the object?

It is seen that the verb is *awoke*, of which the subject (i.e. that which performed the action of the verb) is *telephone*. The object of the verb is *my husband and me*. That part of the object which is a pronoun (i.e. *me*) is correctly in the accusative, because the accusative form of any pronoun (see the table in the previous section) is needed when that pronoun is the object of a verb.

> The telephone awoke my husband and I.

is incorrect, because the nominative form *I* cannot be used as the object of a verb.

> My husband and I awoke early.

is, however, correct; the nominative *I* is here used as part of the subject of a verb.

> Us Welshmen must stick together

is another example of incorrect grammar. One would naturally say

> We must stick together

and the addition of another word (*Welshmen*) to the subject of *must* does not alter the correctness of *We*.

One should be very careful to use the correct form of the pronoun, especially in combinations such as *my brother and I*, *they and their family*, etc.

(*b*)   *Ambiguity*. One sometimes finds sentences such as
> When they finally reached the scene of the crash, they were dead.

The context in which this sentence occurs will presumably make it clear that the first *they* refers to one group of people, e.g. rescuers, and the second *they* to a different group of people, the victims. But the grammar is clumsy, and it is poor style to use the same word twice in quick succession to refer to two different things. There are occasions when looseness in the use of pronouns can produce ambiguity:

The boy told his teacher that he had made a mistake.
does not make clear whether *he* is the teacher or the boy. How would you recast the sentence to show clearly that (a) the boy had made a mistake, (b) the teacher had made a mistake?

(*c*) In the chapter on verbs, it was explained that the verb *to be* does not have an object but a complement (Chapter 4, section 6). This being so, if the verb *to be* is followed by a pronoun, the pronoun should be in the nominative: the accusative form, as used in the object of a verb, would be wrong. Thus

It is she (*not* her) who is to blame.
Strictly speaking, therefore, the common expression *It is me* or *It's me* is ungrammatical, and should be *It is I*. The incorrect form *It's me* is so well established, however, that *It is I* has come to seem almost pedantic, and *It's me* is now acceptable, certainly in everyday use if not in formal circumstances. But *It's me* is not acceptable if it is followed by a clause: thus one must say

It's I who must apologise.
not

It's me who must apologise.

(*d*) *Order of pronouns.*   When pronouns of different persons are used together, the second and the third person precede the first person. Courtesy would suggest such an order. Thus *you and I, he and I, you and we.* The second person precedes the third: *you and she, you and they.* A noun counts as third person: *the neighbours and I, you and the children.*

(*e*) If two or more nouns or pronouns are joined in the subject by *or, nor, either . . . or, neither . . . nor,* the verb of which they are the subject agrees in number (singular or plural) and person with the last-named noun or pronoun in the subject:

Either you or *I am* responsible.
Neither he nor *you are* properly prepared.
Neither you nor *he is* properly prepared.

These forms, though grammatically correct, sound a little awkward, and it is probably best to recast the sentences:

Either *you are* responsible or *I am*.
He is not properly prepared, neither *are you*.
Neither of you *is* ready.

Note that *neither* takes a singular verb.

Exercise 109

Select from the words in brackets the correct one to fill the blank.

1. Uncle Bob took David and . . . to the circus   (I, me).
2. Yes, it's . . . sure enough   (he, him).
3. My daughter and . . . are going on holiday together   (she, her).
4. . . . Englishmen have much to be proud of   (we, us).
5. Our friends and . . . have known each other for years   (they, them).
6. Let John and . . . do it   (I, me).
7. You and . . . make a good partnership   (he, him).

Exercise 110

Rewrite the following, avoiding ambiguity or unpleasant repetition.

1. She quarrelled regularly with her sister, and she returned her sarcasm with insults.
2. The doctor told the patient that his cure lay in his hands.
3. The manager told his assistant that he needed a holiday.

5   The possessive

It will be remembered that the possessive (or *genitive case*) of nouns may be found by adding the apostrophe or *'s*.

The words *my*, *his*, *her*, *its*, *our*, *your*, *their* (and the old-fashioned *thy*) are possessive adjectives: *my career, their freedom*. As such they are used before nouns to indicate the identity of the possessor. They may be described as pronouns in the possessive case, and must be distinguished from possessive pronouns, which are described in the next paragraph.

The words *mine*, *his*, *hers*, *its*, *ours*, *yours*, *theirs* (and the old-fashioned *thine*) are possessive pronouns. They stand for the possessor as well as for that which is possessed. Thus, in

> This is your coat and that one is mine.

the word *mine* not only indicates the possessor of *that one*, but also stands instead of the noun *coat*. Whereas the possessive adjectives described in the last paragraph are always followed by a noun, possessive pronouns serve the double purpose of standing for both possessor and thing possessed, and stand alone without a noun:

> My opinion differs from *yours*.
> It's not your fault, but *theirs*.

Note

(*a*)   no apostrophe is used with pronouns in the possessive case or with possessive pronouns.

(*b*)   *his* and *its* may be used as pronouns in the possessive case or as possessive pronouns: all the rest have different forms (*my, mine ; her, hers*, etc.), though *mine* and *thine* are sometimes found as possessive adjectives in old literature (*mine enemy*; Drink to me only with *thine eyes*).

(*c*)   it is necessary to discriminate between *its* (of it) and *it's* (abbreviation of *it is*). Use *it's* only when the meaning is *it is*: in all other cases use *its*. This is a common source of error.

Exercise 111

Rewrite the following, inserting the apostrophe where necessary.
1. Its a long time since we met.   2. Is this glass yours or mine?
3. She is writing a chapter for a book on womens fashions: hers is about the eighteenth century.   4. Theres no doubt about its accuracy.   5. Theirs is a very difficult job; ours is fairly easy.

6 Some other kinds of pronouns

Read the following:

'This is the oldest part of the castle,' said the guide. 'These are the walls that have confined many a prisoner.'

'What is that strange-looking thing?' asked one visitor, pointing to a wooden frame.

'Those are the stocks,' explained the guide, 'where prisoners were' punished. Anyone who misbehaved was locked in them. The gaolers gave each his turn.'

(a) *This* is the oldest part. *These* are the walls. *Those* are the stocks.

The italicised words are doing the work of nouns. (*This* stands for *This part*. *These* stands for *these walls*). They are called demonstrative pronouns because they point to the place of the person or thing being referred to. *This* and its plural *these* point out things that are near to the speaker. *That* and its plural *those* point to things further away.

Note that *this, that, these* and *those* are not always pronouns. When they are attached to nouns (*this kettle, that machine, these flowers*), they are being used as adjectives, sometimes called demonstrative adjectives (see Chapter 3, section 3). They are only pronouns when they stand instead of a noun.

(b) *What* is that strange-looking thing?

What is used instead of a noun: it is short for *what thing*? It is a pronoun, and because it asks a question it is called an interrogative pronoun. Other words which may be used as interrogative pronouns are *who, whose, whom,* and *which*. Question marks are always needed whenever such pronouns are used interrogatively.

What is not invariably a pronoun. If it describes a noun (*What use is that?*) it is an adjective. The same is true of *whose* and *which* (*Whose car did you come in? Which route did you take?*). These words are only pronouns if they replace nouns. (See Chapter 3, section 3.)

Whom is the accusative form, and must be used as object of a verb:

>Who did it?

but

>Whom do you recommend for captain?

(*c*) *Anyone* who misbehaved.

Anyone is a pronoun which indicates some person (it may sometimes indicate something) without particularising. It is therefore called an indefinite pronoun because it does not say how much or how many or who precisely it refers to. Other indefinite pronouns include *any, some, several, anybody, anything, someone* and *one*. Again these are only pronouns when they stand instead of nouns. Note

>He wrote many books, but *few* are worth reading.   (pronoun)
>*A few* of them are now out of print.   (noun)
>*Few* people now remember the author's name.   (adjective)

(*d*) The gaolers gave *each* his turn.

Each, either, neither and *every* are called distributive pronouns because they have a distinguishing or separating sense: they refer to people or things taken one by one.

It is an important rule of grammar that if any of these pronouns acts as the subject of a verb, the verb must be in the singular:

>Either *is* equally convenient.
>Either of the days *is* equally convenient.
>Neither of the aircraft *carries* many passengers.
>Each of us *has* a chance.

These words may sometimes be used as adjectives:

>*Either day* is convenient.
>*Neither solution* is satisfactory.
>*Each member* has a vote.

(*e*) It is not necessary to remember the names of these categories of pronoun: the categories are simply aids to understanding the various ways in which pronouns can perform their function of standing in place of nouns.

Exercise 112

Say which of the italicised words are pronouns and which are adjectives.

1. *This* is my plan.   2. *This* plan is dangerous.   3. *What* size of shoe do you take?   4. *Which* did you choose?   5. For *whom* will you vote?   6. *Whom* will you vote for?   7. *Which* firm does he work for?   8. *Many* visitors were expected.   9. Did *many* come?   10. *Several* pigeons have been lost.   11. Have you *any*?   12. Is there *any* tea left?

Exercise 113

Supply the correct verb from those in brackets.

1. Neither of the seats . . . comfortable.   (is, are, were)
2. Everyone . . . doing his best.   (is, are, were)
3. Every one of the passengers . . . saved.   (were, was, are)
4. Each of the soldiers . . . taking a risk.   (is, are, were)
5. All the soldiers . . . out today.   (fly, flies)
6. Each buyer . . . losing money.   (risk, risks)
7. Neither method . . . to me.   (appeals, appeal)
8. Either of the suggestions . . . me. (suit, suits)

7   Emphasising and reflexive pronouns

Examine these sentences:

> I'll do the job *myself.*
>
> I've cut *myself* with the tin-opener.

What is the word *myself* doing in both these sentences?

In the first, it is emphasising that I, and no-one else, will do the job. The subject of the sentence is *I*, and *myself* is part of the subject, reinforcing it, as if the sentence were

> *I myself* will do the job.

In the second sentence, however, *myself* is not used for emphasis. It is the object of the verb *cut*, of which *I* is the subject. It refers back to the same person as the subject; it reflects the subject, and is called a reflexive pronoun.

Both emphasising and reflexive pronouns have the same forms: *myself, yourself, himself, herself, itself, ourselves, yourselves, themselves* (not *theirselves*!). That is to say, the singular forms end in *-self* and the plural forms in *-selves*.

It is a common error of spoken and written English to use these pronouns in place of the personal pronouns described in sections 2 and 3. One sometimes hears such uses as

My wife and myself will be glad to come.

I haven't seen your children or yourself for three years.

These are incorrect, and the normal personal pronouns should be used:

My wife and *I* will be glad to come.

I haven't seen your children or *you* for three years.

Pronouns in *-self* and *-selves* should be used only in the two ways described in this section: for emphasis, and in reflexive senses.

Exercise 114

Say which pronouns are emphasising and which reflexive.

1. I shall see him myself.   2. The chief cashier himself did not notice the error.   3. The dinghy righted itself.   4. Look after yourself.   5. The children are very good at amusing themselves.
6. We have often noticed it ourselves.

Exercise 115

Pick out the pronouns in the following.

We had now been in the maze for over three hours. One of the party fancied himself as a guide, but he was lost himself and we were lost with him. He had given each of us instructions to keep close to him. This we had done, but if ever there was an incompetent guide it was ours that day. We took this turning, then that; if somebody remembered that we had passed that way before, we turned round and went back. We kicked ourselves for allowing anyone ever to have brought us into that maze.

8 Relative pronouns

Examine the following:

(i) The shop assistant was an obliging person. She spent a long time helping me.

(ii) The shop assistant was an obliging person and she spent a long time helping me.

(iii) The shop assistant was an obliging person who spent a long time helping me.

All these say exactly the same thing in three different ways.

(i) consists of two sentences.

(ii) is one sentence consisting of two clauses linked by *and*. (You will remember that a clause is a group of words which includes a finite verb and forms part of a sentence.)

(iii) is also one sentence consisting of two clauses. One clause is

The shop assistant was an obliging person

The other clause is

who spent a long time helping me.

Consider the word *who* in (iii). If you compare sentence (iii) with sentence (ii), you will see that *who* replaces *and she*, and does the work of the two words *and* and *she*. The first of these two words is a conjunction (*and*) (see Chapter 8), so *who* performs the joining function of relating one clause to the other. The second of these two words is a pronoun (*she*), so *who* also performs the work of a pronoun. *Who* is called a *relative pronoun* in sentence (iii). The clause it introduces is an adjectival clause describing the noun *person*.

Here is another example.

We drove past a building which had been damaged by fire.

could have been written

We drove past a building *and it* had been damaged by fire.

Clearly, *which* in the first sentence is equal to *and it* in the second. In other words, *which* does the work of the pronoun *it* (in standing for a noun, *building*) and also the work of the conjunction *and* in joining the two clauses. In such a sentence, *which* is a relative pronoun, because it relates one clause to another and also does the work of a pronoun in standing for a noun. The clause it introduces is an adjectival clause, describing the noun *building*.

(i) This is the house. Jack built the house.
(ii) This is the house *and* Jack built *it*.
(iii) This is the house *that* Jack built.

By the reasoning used in previous examples, *that* is a relative pronoun in sentence (iii) because it does the work of a conjunction and a pronoun.

Now consider the following example:

(i) My boss is a cheerful man. Everyone likes my boss.
(ii) My boss is a cheerful man *and* everyone likes *him*.
(iii) My boss is a cheerful man *whom* everyone likes.

The pronoun *whom* in (iii) is doing the work of *and . . . him* in (ii). Note that *him* is in the accusative form because it is the object of the verb *likes*. Therefore it has to be replaced by the accusative form *whom*. In the clause

whom everyone likes

the verb is *likes*, its subject is *everyone* and its object is *whom*. It is an adjectival clause describing the noun *man*

(i) These are the children. The children's dog has got lost.
(ii) These are the children *and their* dog has got lost.
(iii) These are the children *whose* dog has got lost.

The relative pronoun *whose* in (iii) is the possessive form because it replaces *and their*, of which *their* is the possessive form, standing for the possessive *children's*.

It can now be seen that the relative pronoun *who* has the accusative *whom* and the possessive *whose*. It is the only relative pronoun to change in this way. The other relative pronouns *which, that, what* (and sometimes *as*: see section 9) do not change their form, though they may be

(*a*) nominative
   He has sold the business *which* has been in the family for
   many years.

(*b*) accusative
   This is the furniture *which* we shall sell.

(c) possessive
There is a large hall, the ceiling *of which* needs painting.

It is very common in English to omit the relative pronoun when it is the object of a verb:

This is the furniture we shall sell.

Use *who* and *whom* when referring to people. Use *which* when referring to things. (*The person which I told you about* is wrong.) *That* may be applied to persons or things. *Whose* is best reserved for people, but it is becoming common to apply it to things if the alternative *of which* is cumbersome.

Note that the pronouns described in this section are not *invariably* relative pronouns. The word *which*, for example, may be an interrogative pronoun

Which have you chosen?

or an adjective

Which way shall we go?

See section 6(*b*).

Exercise 116

Join the following pairs of sentences by the use of a relative pronoun.

1. It was a poor game. It was watched by only a small crowd.
2. The home team has had a poor season. The home team's supporters are highly critical.
3. The visiting team looked tired. They had had a mid-week match.
4. The referee was kept very busy. He was the object of many coarse comments.
5. The captain of the home team was the best player. The crowd cheered him whenever he got the ball.
6. The referee made the decision to abandon the match because of fog. The crowd noisily objected to the decision.

Exercise 117

Insert either *who* or *whom* in the following.

1. It is always a pleasure to meet old friends . . . one has not seen for many years.
2. He was the last person in the world . . . I expected to meet.
3. The men . . . are employed there are well paid.
4. We must telephone those people . . . we want to invite round for a meal.
5. . . . shall we send?

Exercise 118

Combine each of the following into single sentences. Use relative pronouns or any other suitable means.

1. Suddenly she stamped her foot. At the same time she screamed. Everyone could hear her.
2. She went to her bedroom. It was at the top of the house. She left her husband downstairs.
3. Her husband was the only other occupant of the house. He was a nervous man. He had the task of putting the cat out every night.
4. The wall was exceptionally tall. It was covered with ivy. A burglar alarm had been fitted to it.
5. The police arrived quickly. Their suspicions had already been aroused.

Exercise 119

Pick out the adjectival clauses in the following, stating the relative pronouns that have been omitted.

1. The house we rented was very close to the sea.
2. The person you want is in the office at the end of the corridor.
3. Tennis is the game he likes best.
4. When you have read it, please return it to the library, not to me.
5. The noise the car made stopped everyone in the street.
6. The girl I was with told me I had the most unusual face she had ever seen.

7. I see that you do not understand.
8. What did it say on the road sign we have just passed?

9 Another relative pronoun

The word *as* may be used as a relative pronoun after *such* and *same*, and more occasionally after *as*:

There was *such* a quarrel *as* I never wish to see again.
He made the *same* speech *as* he had made the previous week.
He caught *as* big a fish *as* I have seen for a long time.

In all three sentences, *as* (the second one in the final sentence) introduces adjectival clauses describing *quarrel*, *speech* and *fish* respectively.

10 Pronouns and adjectives

It has been shown at several points in this chapter that a word may be a pronoun in some contexts and an adjective in others.

It should not be difficult to distinguish between these two. A pronoun is used instead of a noun: an adjective describes a noun:

This is your chance.   (Demonstrative Pronoun)
This chance will not recur.   (Adjective)

The following table illustrates the use of the same word as pronoun and adjective:

Kind	Pronoun	Adjective
Possessive	The responsibility is his.	*His* talent is astonishing.
Demonstrative	*Those* were the days!	*Those* colours do not match.
Interrogative	*What* are you doing?	*What* time is it?
Indefinite	Where shall I find *another*?	*Another* crisis has passed.
Distributive	*Each* is acceptable.	Take *each* case on its merits.

Exercise 120

Construct sentences using the following as (*a*) pronouns, (*b*) adjectives.

which, any, either, every, what, whatever, such, that.

Revision

Exercise 121

Write out definitions of the following as fully as you can, and check the accuracy of your answers by reference to the above chapter.

pronoun; the difference between *its* and *it's*; the difference between emphasising and reflexive pronouns; relative pronoun; the use of *who* and *whom*.

Exercise 122

Pick out the relative pronouns in the following.

1. The man who never made a mistake never made anything.
2. These are the prizes which are to be awarded.
3. The actor whom we saw was an understudy.
4. It's one of the proverbs that my mother used to quote.
5. He is as good a swimmer as I've ever seen.
6. I'll catch the same train as you caught last week.
7. All that he said is true.
8. The hotel where we usually stay was full.

Exercise 123

Say whether the italicised word is an adjective or a pronoun.

1. Behave *yourselves*.
2. *Which* one is *yours*?
3. *Whose* baby is *this*?
4. *We* saw *them* yesterday.
5. I shall not go *either*.

7 The Preposition

1 Definition

Consider the following:

They live in a bungalow *near* the village.
They live in a bungalow *in* the village.
They live in a bungalow *beyond* the village.

The three italicised words express three different relationships between the noun *bungalow* and the noun *village*. In the sentences

They live *near* the village.
They live *in* the village.
They live *beyond* the village.

the italicised words express different relationships between the verb *live* and the noun *village*. You will have noticed, of course, that the three sentences are, in each case, identical except for the italicised words; the differences in meaning are attributable to these words, which express different relationships between *village* and the rest of the sentences.

The italicised words are examples of *the preposition*. In the first set of examples above, the prepositions relate two nouns (*bungalow, village*). In the second set of examples, the prepositions relate a verb and a noun (*live, village*). A preposition may also express a relationship between an adjective and a noun:

She is full *of* ideas.
It is blunt *from* over-use.
The army, fighting *for* survival, retreated in good order.

We can see from these examples that a preposition can express a
relationship between noun and noun

> They live in a *bungalow* near *the village.*

between verb and noun

> They *live* near the *village.*

and between adjective and noun

> She is *full* of *ideas.*

You will observe that 'noun' is common to all three. It is important to remember that wherever we say 'noun' we mean 'noun or
pronoun or noun equivalent'. Here is an example of a preposition
relating verb and pronoun:

> Come and sit between us.

As an example of 'noun equivalent', note the noun clause after
the preposition in

> What is his reaction to *what has happened?*

To summarise, a preposition is a word that expresses the relationship between a noun (or pronoun or noun equivalent) and some
other part of the same sentence, which may be a verb, an adjective
or another noun (or pronoun or noun equivalent).

The meaning of the word *preposition* is *placed before.* Thus the
preposition is most commonly (but not always) found before the
noun.

Prepositions are often used in the formation of phrases. In

> They live in a bungalow *near the village.*

the italicised words are an adjectival phrase describing the noun
bungalow and consisting of preposition + noun. In

> They live *near the village.*

the same phrase is an adverbial phrase because it describes the
verb *live.*

Common words which may be used as prepositions include
*at, after, above, along, across, among, around, by, before, below,
beside, beneath, during, down, for, from, in(to), near, on, to,
through, under, with, without.* Many of these words, however,
and many other words which may act as prepositions, may
equally well act as other parts of speech. For example, in

> Shall we swim *across?*

the word *across* is an adverb, describing the verb *swim* by telling
us where the action of the verb is to take place. But in

Shall we swim *across* the lake?

across is doing a different sort of work, relating *lake* to *swim*. Is is therefore a preposition. Note likewise:

Come *along*.

Let's walk *along* this path.

Exercise 124

Supply suitable prepositions to make adjectival phrases in the following.

1. It was the houses . . . the sea-front that met the full blast of the hurricane.
2. The men . . . the mine are in great danger.
3. The pilot . . . the aircraft realised that something was wrong.
4. The shop . . . the corner is for sale.
5. The noise . . . the hall was deafening.

Exercise 125

Supply suitable prepositions to make adverbial phrases.

1. The procession will go . . . the park.
2. The sun disappeared . . . the clouds.
3. He is shaking . . . apprehension.
4. Please come . . . the waiting-room.
5. The squirrel ran . . . the tree, . . . the garden, . . . the hedge and . . . the road.

Exercise 126

Pick out the prepositions and identify the noun (or pronoun or noun equivalent) that is related to

(*a*) a verb:
    1. He writes for a living.
    2. They used to live near us.
    3. We shall not stop on the way.

(*b*) an adjective:
    4. He is proud of his collection.
    5. I will be satisfied with whatever you choose.

(c)   a noun (etc.)

6.   What are you interested in?
7.   The building was a mass of ruins.
8.   I found it in the street.
9.   Please send it to me.
10. I left the car near where we parked yesterday.

Exercise 127

Say whether the italicised words are prepositions or adverbs.

1.   I've seen this film *before*.
2.   It will have to be finished *before* the holidays.
3.   He crawled *underneath* to look for it.
4.   He found it *underneath* the sink.
5.   We are staying *in* tonight.
6.   The patient must remain *in* bed a little longer.
7.   How are you getting *on*?
8.   The man *on* the right of the photograph is his uncle.

2   The object of the preposition

You will remember from the previous chapter that pronouns have different forms depending on whether they are subject or object; thus the pronoun *I* is used as subject (*I miss you*) but becomes *me* in the accusative (*Do you miss me?*). Nouns do not change in this way, but pronouns do.

It is an important rule of English grammar that if a preposition is followed by a pronoun, the pronoun must be in the accusative (i.e. object) form: for a full table of the accusative forms of pronouns, see section 3 of the previous chapter. Thus we say *Give it to me* (not *to I*), *This is for him*, *That depends on them*. The pronouns *me*, *him*, and *them* are the accusative forms of *I*, *he* and *they*, and are necessary after the pronouns *to*, *for* and *on*.

Sometimes, a preposition is followed by *two* pronouns (or a noun and a pronoun) linked by *and*. It is surprising how often errors creep in under such circumstances. Whereas one would instinctively say

> A strange thing happened to *me*.

where *me* is correctly in the accusative after the preposition *to*, one is likely to hear

> A strange thing happened to my husband and *I*.

even though the insertion of *my husband and* makes not the slightest difference to the basic grammatical structure: the preposition still needs the accusative *me*, even though a noun has been inserted after it and linked with the pronoun by *and*:

> A strange thing happened to my husband and me.

That is to say, the preposition *to* governs both *my husband* and *me*; if nouns in English had an accusative form, *my husband* would be accusative, as *me* is.

An even more common error is found in the expression *Between you and I*, which should always be *Between you and me*, because *between* is here acting as a preposition. The pronoun *you* happens to be the same in both accusative and nominative, but in this expression it is in the accusative after the preposition *between*, and the accusative *me* is also needed.

Remember, then, that if a preposition is followed by two pronouns (or a noun and a pronoun), the pronouns must be in the accusative.

You will also remember from the previous chapter (section 8) that the relative pronoun *who* is unique in having an accusative form *whom*. It follows that this form must be used after a preposition:

> They are people *for whom* I have great respect.
>
> *To whom* shall I address it?

In spoken English it is common for the preposition and *whom* to be separated, but the accusative is none the less required:

> They are people *whom* I have great respect *for*.
>
> *Whom* shall I address it *to*?

However, *who* is commonly found in such circumstances, and though it is wrong, it would not now be regarded as a serious error.

Exercise 128

Supply the correct form of the preposition.

1. Our parents gave permission for my brother and . . . to stay out late. (I, me)
2. Is there enough for you and . . . . (he, him)
3. Between you and . . . , I don't think he's to be trusted. (I, me)
4. . . . are you going with? (Who, Whom)
5. . . . were you with last night? (*Who, Whom*)
6. . . . did you meet at the party? (Who, Whom)
7. . . . was it who told you that? (Who, Whom)
8. . . . and her friend are travelling together. (Her, She)
9. The cost has to be shared between . . . and . . . . (they, them/us, we)

3 Other points about prepositions

(*a*) *Whom* is not the only relative pronoun that may be found after a preposition, though it is the only one with a separate accusative form. See section 8 of the previous chapter.

He's retired to the village *in which* he was born.
There will be an interval, *during which* refreshments will be served.

Both of these sentences contain a preposition followed by a relative pronoun. If both sentences are slightly recast, however

He's retired to the village *where* he was born.
There will be an interval, *when* refreshments will be served.

They now contain what are called *relative adverbs* introducing adjectival clauses. The adverbial nature of *where* and *when*, and their 'relating' function, may be seen more clearly by splitting these sentences into their component parts.

He's retired to the village. He was born *there*.
There will be an interval. Refreshments will be served *then*.

The words *there* and *then* are clearly adverbs. When each pair of sentences is run into one, these words have to be changed to *where* and *when* to carry out the joining or relating function. They are still adverbs, but now they are relative adverbs.

(*b*)   It was stated in Chapter 4, section 5, that some verbs may have two objects:

> He lent me his trombone.

Here, the direct object (i.e. what was *lent*) is *trombone*, and *me* (meaning *to me*) is the indirect object.

It can now be seen that the indirect object in such cases is in fact an adverbial phrase consisting of a preposition (sometimes omitted or 'understood') with a pronoun in the accusative.

You will perhaps have noticed already that all prepositional phrases are either adverbial phrases (if the preposition relates a noun/pronoun/noun equivalent to a verb) or adjectival phrases (if the preposition relates a noun to an adjective or to another noun/pronoun/noun equivalent). Thus

> An interested crowd gathered *around the stall*.   (adverbial)
> The salesman was full *of witticisms*.   (adjectival)
> His takings *during the day* must have been considerable. (adjectival)

(*c*)   Some grammar books insist that *between*, as a preposition, can refer to *two* people or things only, and that *among* or *amongst* must be used if more than two are indicated:

> The proceeds were divided between two charities.
> The spoils were shared out among all the members of the gang.

There is little authority for this rule, and it may be ignored.

If *between* is followed by a conjunction, this must be *and*. Logic requires

> The choice lies between travelling quickly but expensively
>   by air *and* slowly but cheaply by train and boat.

In such a sentence, *or* would be wrong because it would duplicate the sense of *between*.

(*d*)   *But* is sometimes used as a preposition, and should in such cases govern the accusative:

> Nobody *but him* can understand how it works.

Because this sounds clumsy (the ear expecting the nominative *he* immediately before the verb *can understand*), it would be regarded as correct to say

> Nobody but he can understand how it works.

on the grounds that *Nobody but he* is a sort of compound subject. subject justifying the nominative *he*.

(*e*)   In longish sentences, grammatical structures sometimes break down. For example,

> It is on Parliament that the country looks for an initiative in the work of developing new industries in depressed areas.

One looks *to* someone, or relies *on* someone. In the above sentence, the preposition *on* is used with the verb *looks*. Either change *on* to *to*, or change *looks* to *relies*.

Similarly,

> To a person of his experience, the task of merging the two businesses will not be a matter of much difficulty to him.

When the writer of this sentence reached the final two words, he had forgotten how he had begun the sentence; the result is the needless repetition of the same idea. The final two words are superfluous and should have been omitted.

Such incorrect uses of prepositions arise through carelessness and can be avoided by a little thought.

(*f*)   'Never use a preposition to end a sentence with' is an old rule of grammar that is so worded as to be an illustration of the error which the rule warns against.

There are certainly occasions when prepositions at the end of sentences are clumsy or even confusing, as in the question which the mother asked her child:

> What did you choose that book to be read to out of for?

There are also occasions when attempts to avoid terminal prepositions produce awkward or stilted sentences:

> That's a job at which you ought to jump.

instead of the more natural

> That's a job you ought to jump at.

Many verbs in our language are commonly used in close connexion with prepositions – to grumble *at*, to work *for*, to put *off*, *on*, *in*, etc. – and indeed some verbs are virtually inseparable from particular prepositions: that being so, any rule insisting that prepositions must be used only within, not at the end of, sentences is bound to cause problems and encourage any writer or speaker to distort the natural order of words.

Ignore the rule, therefore. What matters is clarity and naturalness.

Have you got a box in which I can keep these photographs?
is a little more formal than

Have you got a box which I can keep these photographs in?

but both are correct. To ignore the rule is also to allow mobility to the preposition, resulting in flexibility and variety of expression.

Exercise 129

Improve the following.

1. The new scheme is contrary to the plans previously approved by the Council and with what was urged by the local residents.
2. To me the thought of the destruction of those historic houses gives me great anxiety.
3. This camera is different to yours in many ways.
4. What do you want him to be written to for?
5. Poverty with happiness is more preferable than wealth with sorrow.

4 Correct construction

Certain prepositions are always used with certain words. As is not uncommon in the English language, no definite rules can be given which are applicable to all words, but as the reader meets special combinations of word and preposition he should note them.

Here are a few examples:

(i) *nouns with prepositions:* grudge against, freedom from, enmity with, authority on *or* over, identity with, tendency to.

(ii) *adjectives with prepositions:* similar to, conscious of, different from (*not* to) preferable to, typical of, synonymous with, ashamed of, averse from (*or* to), worthy of, opposite to, independent of, compared *with* or *to*.

(iii) *verbs with prepositions:* prevail against, prevent from, acquiesce with, agree to (a thing) *or* with (a person), compensate for, aim at, congratulate on, differ from, suffer from (*not* with)

Exercise 130

Construct sentences containing the following words followed by appropriate prepositions.

(a) *Nouns* 1. parody 2. thirst 3. suspicion 4. bias 5. heir
(b) *Adjectives* 6. full 7. opposite 8. dependent 9. contemporary 10. averse
(c) *Verbs* 11. digress 12. approve 13. vie 14. derive 15. delve

Exercise 131

Insert the correct preposition.
1. She has a taste . . . poetry.
2. The cheese tasted . . . paraffin.
3. My son corresponds . . . a French pen-friend.
4. This piece corresponds . . . that.
5. The librarian is an authority . . . early printed books.
6. The leaders are failing to exercise authority . . their members.
7. They shared a degree . . . common sense.
8. She has a degree . . . economics.
9. They will be accompanied . . . their children.
10. He returned the faulty article, accompanied . . . a letter of complaint.

Revision

Exercise 132

Write out a full definition of the preposition, then check the accuracy of what you have written by referring to the above chapter.

Exercise 133

Insert either *past* (a preposition) or *passed* (a verb) in the following.

1. The road goes . . . the cemetery.
2. That's the car that . . . us earlier.
3. It's nearly half . . . five.
4. He's just . . . his driving test.

Exercise 134

What part of speech is *past* in the following.

1. There's a post-office just past the toy-shop.
2. He's just gone past the window.
3. He's just gone past.
4. The past is best forgotten.
5. What is a past participle?

Exercise 135

State whether the italicised words are prepositions or adverbs.

1. What time did you get *up*?
2. If she finds out she'll go *up* the wall.
3. Is the water-heater switched *on*?
4. Is he getting *on* all right?
5. It's further down *on* the right.
6. The fire started *underneath* the stage.
7. *Underneath* he found an unopened letter.

8. He succeeded *through* his own efforts.
9. Push it *through* and screw it *in*.
10. 'Come *along with* me,' said the nurse, walking *off along* the corridor.

Exercise 136

Construct sentences using *down* as:

(*a*) noun   (*b*) adjective   (*c*) verb   (*d*) adverb   (*e*) preposition

Exercise 137

Write sentences using the following as (i) prepositions, (ii) adverbs.

1. across   2. above   3. over   4. under   5. off   6. near   7. in   8. around

Exercise 138

Write sentences using the verb *put* with as many different prepositions as you can think of.

Exercise 139

Which prepositions normally follow

1. different   2. preferable   3. hostile   4. indifferent   5. compatible

8 The Conjunction and Interjection

1 The conjunction: definition

A junction is a joining, or a place where things join: a railway junction is a place where two or more railway lines join. It is sometimes necessary to have a junction between words: gin *and* tonic, slowly *but* surely, *neither* here *nor* there. Can you suggest other common expressions of this kind?

The joining words are called *Conjunctions*. They may link single words

I've forgotten my pipe *and* matches.

or phrases

He ignored the noise of the engines *and* the shouts of the crowd.

or clauses

We must hurry *or* we shall be late.

This last example shows two sentences joined by a conjunction to form one sentence of two clauses.

Exercise 140

Say whether the conjunctions are joining clauses, phrases or single words.

1. The vans carried assorted meats *and* clothes, groceries, furniture, hardware *and* haberdashery.
2. The men who drove them knew their way about *and* enjoyed their knowledge.

3. To the delivery drivers *and* to all the neighbours he was a familiar figure.
4. They could tell you a thing or two, *but* they probably never would.
5. He was greeted without respect *but* without ill-will either.

Exercise 141

Pick out the conjunctions and state their function.

1. Look before you leap.
2. It is quite clear that they are going to lose.
3. I'll come if I can.
4. The storm burst before we could find shelter.
5. Monday or Tuesday will suit me.
6. He has not been affected by criticism in the press nor by threats of legal action.

Exercise 142

Join the following sentences by using conjunctions.

1. Swallows migrate in winter. Robins stay during the whole year.
2. The courts are under water. We cannot play tennis.
3. He has no friends. He does not seem to want any.
4. We are looking forward to Christmas. We are going away for a few days.

Exercise 143

Supply suitable conjunctions.

1. The magistrate spoke kindly . . . firmly.
2. He is thirteen . . . fourteen years old.
3. I can't leave . . . the job is finished.
4. She opened the door . . . I had time to knock.
5. He scored 70 . . . his partner was making 15.
6. . . . he is very young, he is an experienced chess-player.

7. Tell him . . . we are in a hurry.
8. No one will buy it . . . the price is reduced.

2 The conjunction: some problems

(*a*) Words commonly used as conjunctions include *although, and, as, after, before, because, but, if, nor, or, since, though, than, that, till, until, unless, whereas, yet.*

As always, words in English can be different parts of speech in different contexts. What matters above all is the function of a word in a *particular* sentence. Thus the word *after* can be a conjunction

> It happened *after* I arrived.

or a preposition

> The damage *after* the earthquake was extensive.

or an adverb

> I only found out *after*.

(*b*) The following illustrates a common error:

> Scarcely had the plane taken off *than* engine-failure occurred.

In such constructions, *scarcely* should be followed by *when*, not *than*.

(*c*) One often hears the expression *try and* in such contexts as

> Try and see if they've any in stock.

which means

> Try to find out if they've any in stock.

It is best to use *try to*, not *try and*, in such circumstances, because *try to* is more logical. It can be argued that *try and* is preferable if the intention is to encourage, so that

> He was told to try and succeed.

carries the shade of meaning of

> He was told to try – and he would succeed.

whereas

> He was told to try to succeed.

sounds more like an order.

(*d*) The words *like* and *except* cannot be used as conjunctions. Problems often arise with *like*: it may be used as a preposition

> The infection spread like wildfire.

but never as a conjunction. Thus

> He is a hard worker like his father was.

should have *as* instead of *like*. A less common error is to use *except* as a conjunction:

> You won't get in except you book in advance.

should have *unless* instead of *except*.

Exercise 144

Say whether the italicised words are prepositions or conjunctions.

1. He is honest *but* indecisive.   2. He thinks of nobody *but* himself.   3. *After* lunch we'll go for a walk.   4. *After* we've finished lunch, we'll go for a walk.   5. He has been abroad *since* last month.   6. Have you heard from him *since* he went abroad?

Exercise 145

Identify the italicised parts of speech.

1. Nothing has been heard of him *since*.
2. He waited *until* dark.
3. He waited *until* it was dark.
4. Had you met him *before*?
5. Had you met him *before* this evening?
6. Did you see him *before* he left?
7. She felt embarrassed *that* he had behaved in *that* way.
8. I find it hard to believe *that*.

3   The interjection: definition

There are occasions when we express some sudden feeling or sentiment, often without thinking, sometimes as an exclamation.

Quite a lot of feelings are communicated, especially in everyday speech, in the form of 'Oh!' and 'Ah!' – both of which can be given many shades of meaning. Agreement and disagreement can be expressed by 'Mm!', surprise by 'Well!', regret by a sound normally written as 'Tut, tut!', relief by 'Whew!' and disgust by 'Bah!'.

These are called *Interjections*, and are often found at the beginnings of sentences to express joy, sorrow, surprise, dismay or some other emotion. Interjections may be in the form of single words or sounds (*Sh! Well!*), or phrases (*What a pity! Oh dear!*) or sentences (*I say!*).

Interjections are usually followed by exclamation marks (!). Grammatically, they have no part in the construction of a sentence, and are to be regarded simply as additions. Thus, in

Really! I don't believe it!

I is the subject, *don't believe it!* is the predicate, and *Really!* is an interjection which does not affect the grammar in any way. Nowadays, the exclamation mark is often omitted, or postponed:

Hello, what's happening?
Well, that is a surprise!

Exercise 146

Construct sentences using interjections to express surprise, dismay, elation, doubt, reproof.

9   A Revision Chapter

1   Case

In the previous chapter, there have been several references to
case. In the chapter on the noun (Chapter 2, section 5) it was
explained that the possessive forms of nouns is sometimes referred to as the *genitive case*:

> The windows look like *a ship's* port-holes.   (singular)
> *Nurses'* working-hours are to be reduced.   (plural)

Pronouns too are found in the genitive case: *his* coat, *our*
problem.

In the chapter on the verb (Chapter 4) there were references
to the *nominative case* (section 2) and the *accusative case* (section
3).   A word or group of words is said to be in the nominative
case if it acts as the subject of a verb, and in the accusative if it
acts as object.

In some old grammar books, you may come across two other
cases. The indirect object (see Chapter 4, section 5, and Chapter
7, section 3(b)) is sometimes called the *dative case*. When a noun
is used in such a way as to denote that someone is being spoken
to

> I'm very glad to see you, *Philip*.
> *Ladies and gentlemen*, shall we begin?

it is said to be in the *vocative case*. These two terms are now no
longer used, and need not be memorised.

It is worth remembering the terms *nominative* and *accusative*, but 'possessive form *or* case' is more common than *genitive*, and 'indirect object' is certainly more common than *dative*.

For revision purposes, here is a table showing the cases of a noun (*driver*) and a pronoun (*he*).

	Singular		Plural
Nominative	Driver	*The driver was too impatient.*	Drivers
	He	*He was too impatient.*	They
Accusative	Driver	*I blame the driver.*	Drivers
	Him	*I blame him.*	Them
Possessive	Driver's	*The driver's haste caused the accident.*	
			Drivers'
	His	*His haste caused the accident.*	Their
Indirect Object	Driver	*The court gave the driver a heavy fine.*	Drivers
	Him	*The court gave him a heavy fine.*	Them

Exercise 147

Write sentences illustrating the use of the nominative

1. as subject of a sentence
2. as subject of a clause within a sentence
3. as a complement
4. as part of an Absolute Construction.

Exercise 148

Write sentences illustrating the use of the accusative

1. as object of a verb
2. as object of a preposition
3. as object of a verb in a clause within a sentence.

Exercise 149

Write sentences illustrating the use of

1. the indirect object

2. a plural noun in the possessive case
3. a singular pronoun in the possessive case.

2 Exercises on all the parts of speech

Exercise 150

Comment on the grammar of the words in italics.

1. God *save* the Queen.
2. *Seeing* is believing.
3. *Agreement having been reached*, the men returned to work.
4. *Whose* is this coat?
5. Will you please take this for *him*?
6. I bought it at the local *grocer's*.
7. They collapsed, *exhausted* by all their efforts.
8. He thinks it will be cheaper to do the job *himself*.
9. Is this the car *which* is for sale?
10. The staff gave *him* a very attractive leaving-present.
11. It was a *courageous* act.
12. The ferry *leaves* at half past four tomorrow afternoon.
13. The disease is spreading with *alarming* speed.
14. He is a *rather* inconsistent player.
15. The agreement should lead to *peace* in the near future.
16. The crowds *cheered* until they were hoarse.
17. He decided to stroll *through the churchyard*.
18. They blame *themselves*.
19. They walked carefully *along* the plank *to* the shore.
20. Sailings have been cancelled *because* there is a heavy storm at sea.
21. *Good heavens*, is that so?
22. *Although it was only five o'clock*, the shops were all closed.
23. It is a *bigger* school than it used to be.
24. *Smoking* can damage your health.
25. The car *he was driving* belongs to his brother.

3 Correct construction

Exercise 151

Rewrite the following correctly.

1. Handwriting is rarely taught today unless to very young children.
2. Everyone of us have to bring our lunch and tea with us.
3. He was the kind of man to constantly quarrel with the likes of you and I.
4. Of the four different schemes for replanning the town centre, the latter is the more ambitious.
5. In a large factory, many matters concerning the welfare of workers are often overlooked, which, if they were implemented, the factory would be a happier place.
6. I've been lain up in bed with lumbago.
7. He is the most attractive of all his brothers, and the most well-dressed.
8. Let my wife and I help you with the preparations.
9. He said that if he had to choose between a light post in which he had little responsibility or a heavy post in which he had heavy responsibility, he would choose the latter.
10. I have entered for the competition but I do not think I will win.
11. This village is the only one of all the other villages in the valley not to have mains electricity.
12. He is one of those men who dislikes complaining.
13. It was a fine goal, and the spectators exalted.
14. Being co-directors, a decision could not be taken without the agreement of all of them.
15. The shape of the building is very unique.
16. It was him that the blow was aimed at.
17. He has now reached the top of the tree in his profession, and from now on he will have plain sailing.
18. The whole story centres round the private life of a successful politician.
19. While walking through the park with his family, a tree only fell down a few yards away from him.

20. Surely you can behave as one likes in his own home.
21. He is the man whom everyone hoped would get the job.
22. Are either of the shops likely to be open at this time of night?
23. Nobody but I and you knows the real reason.
24. None of my friends are likely to be there.
25. He is a mechanic whom we know is reliable.

Exercise 152

Write definitions of the following, then refer to the appropriate sections to check the accuracy of your definitions:

sentence, phrase, clause, transitive and intransitive verb, finite and infinite verb, complement, participle, gerund, comparative and superlative, adverb, adverbial clause, pronoun, relative pronoun, preposition, conjunction, active and passive.

10 Analysis of the Simple Sentence

1 Subject and predicate

It was explained in Chapter 1 that every sentence can be divided into two parts:

(1) The subject, i.e. the part that names what we are thinking about.

(2) The predicate, i.e. the part that makes a statement about the subject.

Examples:

(1) I enjoyed it.

Subject	Predicate
I	enjoyed it

(2) Several thousand people, including many tourists from overseas, were there.

Subject	Predicate
Several thousand people including many tourists from overseas	were there

(3) I have never seen so many people at a fireworks display.

Subject	Predicate
I	have never seen so many people at a fireworks display

Consider the first sentence again: *I enjoyed it.*

Subject: I

Predicate: enjoyed it.

The predicate has two ideas:

       1.   the verb *enjoyed*
       2.   the object of the verb, *it.*

We can represent this in diagrammatic form:

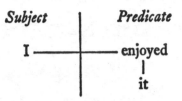

The relationship between subject and verb is indicated by a horizontal line. The division between subject and predicate is indicated by the vertical line in the middle of the page. The relationship between the verb and its object is indicated by a shorter vertical line underneath the verb, suggesting the action of the verb passing over to the object *it.*

    Let us now consider a slightly longer sentence:

    Delighted crowds applauded the spectacle enthusiastically.

Here the noun in the subject, *crowds*, is described by the adjective *delighted*. The verb in the predicate, *applauded*, is described and expanded by the adverb *enthusiastically*. This too can be represented in a diagram

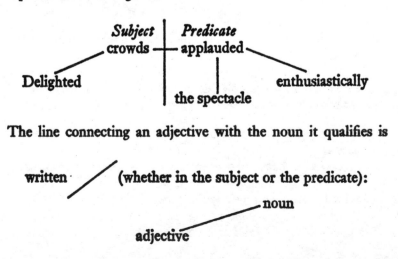

The line connecting an adjective with the noun it qualifies is

and the line connecting an adverb with the verb it qualifies is

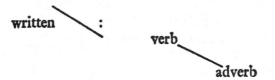

The division of a sentence in this way is called graphic analysis: by it we can show clearly how the component parts of a sentence are linked. There are other methods of showing analysis, but this is perhaps the simplest.

2 Further steps in analysis

It is suggested that the analysis of a sentence should be undertaken by taking the following steps.

Sentence: *Suddenly, a loud noise startled the enormous crowd.*

(i) Find the finite verb: *startled.*

(ii) Find the subject word. Remember that one can find the subject by asking who or what performed the action of the verb. Who or what startled? *noise.*

(iii) We can now set out the basic structure.

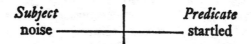

(iv) Are there any words describing the subject? *A loud.* (Note that the indefinite articles *a* and *an*, and the definite article *the*, have an adjectival sense.)

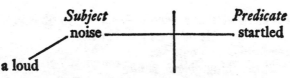

(v) Is there an object of the verb? Remember that the object can be identified by asking who or what receives or suffers the action of the verb. Startled whom or what? *crowd.*

(vi) Are there any words describing the object? *the enormous*.

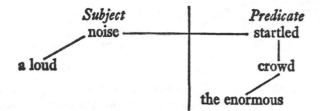

(vii) What remains in the sentence? *Suddenly* – an adverb telling us more about the verb. The final analysis is

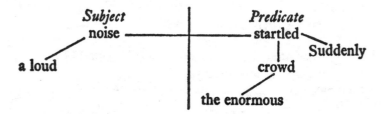

Exercise 153

Do graphic analyses of the following.

1. They agreed.   2. Mirrors reflect light.   3. Several people believed it.   4. The sun is shining brightly.   5. Few travellers visit that dismal place.   6. The lecturer explained the problem clearly.   7. Two light aircraft collided yesterday.   8. Huge waves battered the stricken ship incessantly.

3   Analysis: the indirect object

You will remember that a verb may have two objects:

He gave us good advice

The verb *gave* has two objects:

      (i) the thing given: *advice*

      (ii) the person to whom the thing is given: *us*

The 'thing given' is the *direct object*: remember always to ask 'who or what receives the action of the verb?'

The other object is called the *indirect object*, because it denotes a person or thing *for whom* or *to whom* an action is done. Thus, in the above example, the sense is

He gave (to) us good advice.

The indirect object is represented in graphic analysis thus:

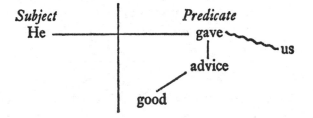

Exercise 154

Give graphic analyses of the following.

1. His wife told him the news. 2. His colleagues bought him a retirement present. 3. All passengers must show the inspector their tickets. 4. We bought all the groceries yesterday. 5. A helpful motorist gave him a lift. 6. They have sent all their customers a reminder.

4 Analysis: the complement

Examine the sentences

(i) Peter has seen a dentist.
(ii) Peter is a dentist.

In the first sentence, the word *dentist* is the direct object of the verb *has seen*. The words *Peter* and *dentist* stand for different persons.

In the second sentence, the nouns *Peter* and *dentist* denote the same person. This sentence is built up as follows:

(i) Subject: *Peter*

(ii) Verb: *is*

(iii) A noun in the predicate: *dentist*. This is called a predicative noun referring to the subject. It helps to complete the sense of the predicate, because *Peter is* by itself does not make complete sense.

A predicative word is usually called the *complement*, because it is needed to complete the sense of the verb (see also Chapter 4, Section 6). In a similar way, an adjective may complete the sense of the verb in the predicate:

> Peter is hard-working.
> The fruit was plentiful.

The adjectives *hard-working* and *plentiful* are predicative adjectives or complements. Here are further examples.

> (i) The wheel turned *slowly*.
> (ii) The driver turned *the wheel*.
> (iii) The defendant turned *pale*.

In the three predicates

(i) *slowly* is an adverb describing how the wheel turned.

(ii) *the wheel* is the direct object of the verb *turned*.

(iii) *pale* is an adjective describing *defendant* and is a predicative adjective referring to the subject. It is therefore a complement.

For the purposes of graphic analysis, the predicative words or complement are shown as a continuation of the verb because they are continuing and completing its sense:

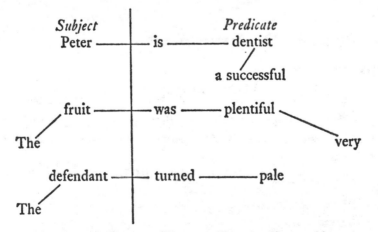

Note that a complement (like a subject, a direct object or an indirect object) may have words describing it. In the above, *successful* is an adjective, and *very* is an adverb describing the adjective *plentiful*. The lines ╱ and ╲ are used accordingly.

Exercise 155

Supply suitable predicative nouns to complete the sense.

1. Peter is . . . 2. Peter became . . . 3. Peter was made . . .
4. He must be . . . 5. He can be . . .

Exercise 156

Supply suitable predicative adjectives to complete the sense.

1. The sea may be . . . 2. The climb was becoming . . . 3. His responsibility is . . . 4. The bus was . . . 5. The night will be . . .

Exercise 157

Say whether the italicised words are direct objects, adverbs or complements.

1. His parents are growing *old*. 2. The farmers are growing more *barley* these days. 3. The children are growing very *quickly*. 4. Motorists are advised to sound their *horns*. 5. It sounds too *easy*. 6. It's so cold I can't feel my *fingers*. 7. I feel *cold*. 8. I feel better *today*. 9. Get *up*. 10. Let's get our *coats*. 11. Don't get *alarmed*. 12. *Suddenly* it stopped. 13. It stopped *dead*. 14. We must try to stop *it*. 15. She seemed very *nervous*. 16. He *always* seems *tired*.

Exercise 158

Analyse the following graphically.

1. Britain is an island. 2. He is becoming powerful. 3. Such a heavy punishment seems inappropriate. 4. The government will almost certainly consider retaliation. 5. Their relationship turned sour. 6. His last symphony is considered his best.

7. His handwriting is becoming small and cramped. 8. He appeared relaxed and confident.

5 Analysis: questions

So far, we have considered the analysis of sentences that take the form of statements. You will remember from Chapter 1, however, that sentences may also take the form of questions.

(*a*) Consider the following sentences:

Who invented wireless telegraphy?
Marconi invented wireless telegraphy.

In these two sentences, the verb is the same: *invented*. The direct object is also the same: who or what was invented? *wireless telegraphy*. The difference between the sentences is that in the second sentence we are told who carried out the action described in the verb: *Marconi* is therefore the subject of this sentence. In the first sentence, *who*, introducing the question, has to stand for an unknown person who carried out the action described in the verb *invented*. *Who* is the subject, and is an interrogative pronoun.

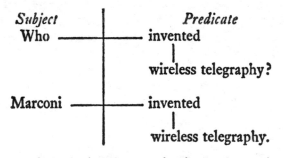

(*b*) The word introducing the question is not always the subject. It may be the object.

He is reading the newspaper.
What is he reading?

In both sentences, *he* is carrying out the action of reading, and is the subject of both sentences. In the first sentence, *newspaper* is the object because it is the thing being read. In the second sentence, *what* is the unknown thing that is being read, and is therefore the direct object of is *reading*.

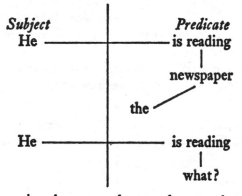

(*c*) Some questions have complements because they contain the verb *to be* (with all its parts *I am, you are, he/she/it is, we are, they are,* and all its tenses) or other verbs which usually need predicative words to complete the sense (see Exercise 157 for some of them).

His name is Henry.
His name is what?
What is his name?

In all three cases, the subject of *is* is *his name*: *Henry* and *what* (whether at the beginning or end of the sentence) are predicative words necessary to complete the sense. As complements, they are graphically represented as continuations of the verb:

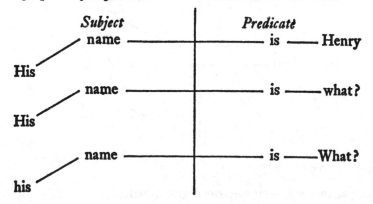

(*d*)   Consider the sentences

   The family is travelling tomorrow.

   When is the family travelling?

In both sentences, the verb is *is travelling*. Who is travelling? *the family*. The adverb *tomorrow* tells when the action of the verb takes place. The word *when* in the second sentence has the same adverbial function: it is an interrogative adverb, asking rather than telling the time when the verb takes place.

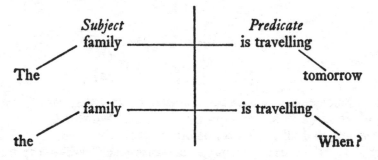

(*e*)   Some questions are merely rearrangements of the order of words in statements. *Can you drive a car?* is an inversion of *You can drive a car*. Subject, verb, object are the same in both. Only the punctuation differs:

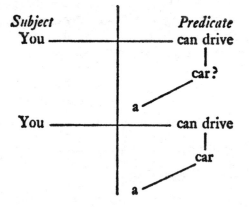

Exercise 159

Analyse the following questions graphically.

1. Who knocked it over? 2. What are you doing? 3. Whom do you want? 4. How did they manage? 5. Where is he going? 6. Why did they never come? 7. Don't you recognise me? 8. When is the next delivery expected? 9. Why did the referee not stop the game earlier? 10. What price did he offer you?

6 Analysis: commands

It was explained in Chapter 1 (and in Chapter 4, section 11(b)) that commands do not have subjects. In, for example,

> Go carefully.
> Watch out!

The action of the verbs is to be performed by an unspecified 'you' who is the person (or persons) to whom the 'command' is given:

> (You must) go carefully.
> (You must) watch out.

The subject is said to be understood, and is represented in graphic analysis in brackets:

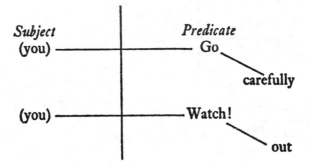

Subject	Predicate
(you) ————————	Go.
	carefully
(you) ————————	Watch!
	out

It may be that the person who is being 'commanded' is named:

> Do sit down, Mrs Bracegirdle.

The subject is still an understood *you*, however, and the sentence is represented

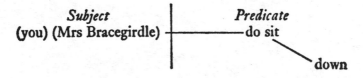

Subject	Predicate
(you) (Mrs Bracegirdle) ———	do sit
	down

Exercise 160

Analyse the following commands graphically.
1. Stop!   2. Mind your heads!   3. Don't do that.   4. Ask me again later.   5. Give him another.

7   Analysis: exclamations

The following exclamations
> What a fuss she made!
> What a mess it all is!

are graphically analysed as follows:

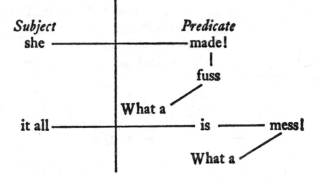

If the sentence contains exclamatory words such as 'Oh', 'Well', etc., these are not part of the grammatical structure of the sentence, and may be omitted from analysis.

Exercise 161

Give graphic analyses of:
1. What a noise they were making!   2. What a nuisance it will be!   3. How they cheered!

Revision

Exercise 162

Analyse the following graphically.

1. How did the car behave?
2. What is the problem now?
3. Be careful!
4. What's up?
5. Give me a ring later this evening.
6. She didn't seem very well.
7. The later models have five gears.
8. Can you see it yet?
9. The lighthouse-keeper, his wife and his daughter were imprisoned.
10. It was a large, rambling, wooden building.
11. Some boys were wearing jerseys and long trousers.
12. Which bus did you catch?
13. He is an extremely helpful person.
14. Show the librarian the torn page.
15. Numerous friends have shown him great kindness recently.

Exercise 163

Write definitions of the following terms, then check the correctness of what you have written by referring to the chapter:

complement, predicative noun, direct object, subject, predicate, indirect object.

11   Equivalents

1   Introduction

We have seen that the simple sentence can be analysed graphically according to the following pattern

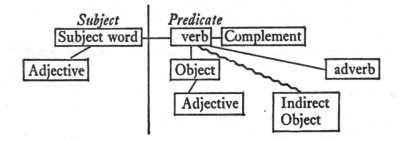

More adjectives could be added to this model, because both complements and indirect objects may have adjectives applied to them.

Not every sentence conforms to this model, of course: it is possible for a verb to exist without an object, direct or indirect, and without a complement.

It is now necessary to approach the analysis of longer sentences. We begin with sentences which contain not only adjectives, adverbs and nouns, but also *groups* of words that do the work of these three parts of speech.

2 Adjectival equivalents

It has been seen earlier in this book that a noun may be described by an adjectival phrase or an adjectival clause. A fuller explanation now follows, showing adjectives in the subject of sentences, in the object and in the complement.

(*a*) In the subject.
  Consider the following sentences:
      (i) The *first* spectators secured good seats.
The subject *spectators* is described by the adjective *first*. However, the writer may wish to express himself differently:
      (ii) The spectators *first to arrive* secured good seats.
The italicised group of words is a phrase, because it does not contain a finite verb (*to arrive* is an infinitive). It is obviously doing the same sort of work as *first* in sentence (1). It is an adjectival phrase describing the subject-word *spectators*.
  Alternatively, one may write
  (iii) The spectators *who were the first to arrive* secured good
        seats.
Again we have a group of words describing the noun *spectators*. This group of words, however, has a subject (who) and a predicate (were the first to arrive); the verb *were* has a subject *who*, and is therefore finite. The group of words is a clause, i.e. a group of words containing a finite verb and enclosed within a longer sentence. Because it is the equivalent of an adjective, it is an adjectival clause describing *spectators*.
  A clause of this sort is sometimes called a *dependent clause* (or subordinate clause) because it depends on the rest of the sentence in order to make sense. The words
              who were the first to arrive
do not make complete sense. If they were equipped with a capital letter and punctuation at the end, the same words could be expressed as a question and make complete sense as the sentence
              Who were the first to arrive?
But in the illustration we are using, they are not used in this

way, but as part of a larger sentence. They *depend* on the rest of the sentence (*The spectators . . . secured the best seats*) in order to make sense.

The three sentences quoted could be graphically analysed as follows:

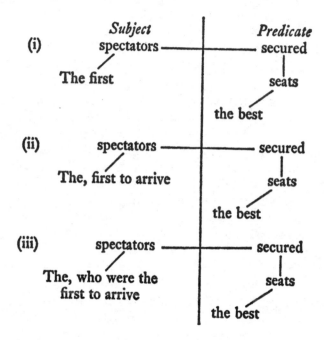

The adjectival equivalents, whether phrase or clause, are joined to the subject by / exactly as the adjective is.

(*b*)   In the object.
In exactly the same way, a noun which is the object of a verb may be described by an adjectival phrase or an adjectival clause.
    (i) Have you met our *Canadian* friends?   (adjective)
   (ii) Have you met our friends *from Canada*?   (adjectival phrase)
  (iii) Have you met our friends *who come from Canada*? (adjectival clause)

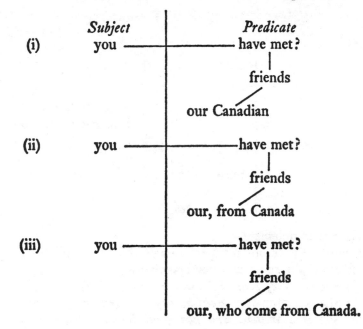

An adjectival phrase or clause may be found in the indirect object:

    (iv) They gave our visitors from Canada a warm welcome.
    (v) He showed our children, who are very interested in sailing, his newly acquired boat.

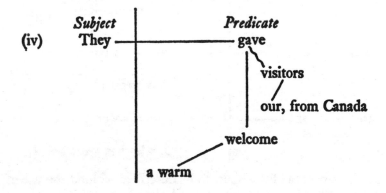

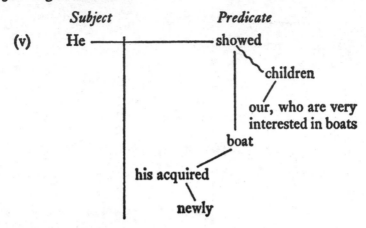

(v)   He ——————— showed

children

our, who are very
interested in boats

boat

his acquired

newly

(*c*)   In the complement.

A noun in the complement may be described by an adjective,
an adjectival phrase or an adjectival clause:

    (i) She is a very *beautiful* woman.   (adjective)
    (ii) She is a woman *of great beauty*.   (adjectival phrase)
    (iii) She is a woman *who has great beauty*.   (adjectival clause)

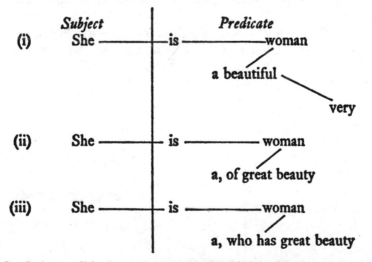

(i)   She ——— is ——————woman

a beautiful

very

(ii)   She ——— is ——————— woman

a, of great beauty

(iii)   She ——— is ——————woman

a, who has great beauty

(*d*)   It is possible for a noun to be described without the use of
an adjective, adjectival phrase or adjectival clause. Consider:

The man, *a retired journalist*, was arrested yesterday.

The italicised words refer to the word *man*, and are said to be *in apposition to* it. They are an enlargement of the subject. A noun in apposition occurs when there are two nouns both referring to the same person or thing. Another example, this time showing a noun in apposition to the direct object:

They have appointed the youngest candidate, *a Yorkshireman*.

For the purposes of graphic analysis, such words in apposition are best regarded as adjectival equivalents.

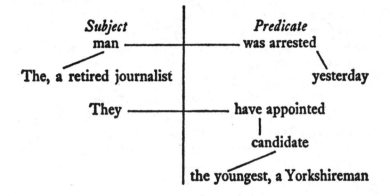

Exercise 164

Substitute nouns or noun phrases in apposition for adjectival clauses.

1. I am reading a book by Hardy, who is my favourite author.
2. My brother, who was an architect, was older than me.
3. Leningrad, which used to be the capital of Russia, is an exceptionally beautiful city.
4. The side includes four Welsh players who are very experienced.
5. Our local councillor, who will be mayor next year, is a farmer.

Exercise 165

Analyse the following graphically.

1. The shop in the High Street has been taken over.
2. The clown with the trumpet was the most popular.
3. The building, which stands on the crest of the hill, is magnificently situated.
4. We suddenly understood the problem that confronted us.
5. The bomb-disposal expert, an officer of many years' experience, defused the explosive device successfully and quickly.
6. Are you sure?
7. The search-party, overcome with fatigue, abandoned their efforts.
8. Shouting wildly, they attacked.
9. The route you suggested was very picturesque.
10. I shall never forget the day when we moved house.
11. He was a general whose moods were unpredictable.
12. The butcher whom you recommended has gone bankrupt.
13. I know a pub where the beer is excellent.
14. I told him the reason why I didn't want it.
15. He became a very popular figure.

3   Adverbial equivalents

Just as a noun may be described by an adjective, an adjectival phrase or an adjectival clause, a verb may be described by an adverb, an adverbial phrase or an adverbial clause. Here are some examples:

He behaved *predictably*.   (adverb, describing the manner in which he behaved)

He behaved *in a predictable fashion*.   (adverbial phrase)

He behaved *as one would have predicted*.   (adverbial clause)

All the italicised expressions are doing the same work in different ways: telling us more about the verb *behaved*. They tell us *how* he behaved.

In graphic analysis, an adverbial phrase or adverbial clause is linked to the verb it qualifies in the same way as an adverb is:

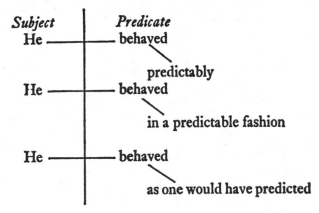

The adverb and adverbial equivalents in the above example described *how* the verb took place. An adverb or adverbial equivalent may also indicate *when* the verb took place:

I awoke *early*.   (adverb of time)
I awoke *at first light*.   (adverbial phrase)
I awoke *as the day was dawning*.   (adverbial clause of time)

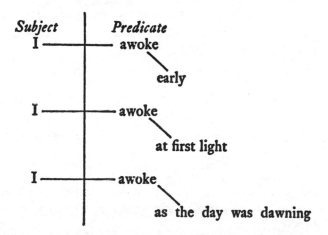

Similarly, an adverb or adverbial equivalent may describe *where* the verb in the predicate took place:

The accident happened *here*.   (adverb of place)
The accident happened *at that corner*.   (adverbial phrase)
The accident happened *where the road bends sharply to the left*.   (adverbial clause of place)

All the italicised expressions answer the question *where?*

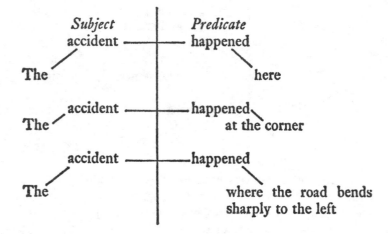

Exercise 166

Provide adverbial phrases equivalent to the following interrogative adverbs. (E.g. the interrogative adverb *when?* can be expressed in the phrase *at what time?* Thus *When will you arrive?* or *At what time will you arrive?*)

1. Where?   2. How?   3. Why?

Exercise 167

Write the sentences using the following phrases as

(*a*)   adverbial equivalents
(*b*)   adjectival equivalents
(E.g. the phrase *at the top of the hill* is used adverbially in *They live at the top of the hill* and adjectivally in *The house at the top of the hill is for sale*.)

1. round the corner   2. in the street   3. with a broken nose
4. across the fields   5. near the wall.

Exercise 168

Analyse the following graphically.

1. The visitors drove away.   2. The trawlers left the harbour at dusk.   3. By midnight, the storm was raging fiercely.   4. They parted at the park-gates.   5. A warning light shows when the oil pressure falls.   6. Leave it where you found it.   7. Where have you been since we last met?   8. You must hold the bow as you have been taught to do.   9. How did you find out so quickly?   10. With the approach of summer, the nights are getting longer and longer.

4 Noun equivalents

Consider the following:

> Do you know the route?
> Do you know where to go?
> Do you know if this is the right road?

In all these three sentences, the verb (*do know*) is the same, and the subject (*you*) is the same. The direct object of the verb in the first sentence is the noun *route*; the direct object in the second sentence is the phrase *where to go*; in the third sentence the object is the clause *if this is the right road*, this clause having a finite verb *is* with its subject *this*.

Thus, it is possible for a phrase or clause to act as a noun equivalent. The above examples show noun equivalents as the direct object; noun equivalents can also stand instead of nouns as the subjects of verbs, as the complements or in apposition. Fuller details are to be found in the following chapter.

In graphic analysis, noun equivalents are placed in the same positions as nouns:

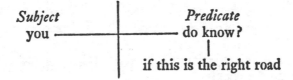

Subject		*Predicate*
you		do know?
		if this is the right road

Exercise 169

Replace the words in italics by suitable noun clauses.

1. Tell me *your opinion*.   2. Has he confessed *his guilt*?   3. Do you know *his expected time of arrival*?   4. The teacher has explained *how to solve the problem*.   5. Ask him *the way*.

Exercise 170

Replace the noun clauses by nouns or noun equivalents.

1. The Prime Minister decides when a general election takes place.
2. Can you tell me what the time is?
3. The farmer knew where the best grazing was to be found.
4. The owner described how the drains worked.
5. The children discovered where their friends were hidden.

Exercise 171

Analyse the following graphically.

1. Their uncle often visits them.   2. Tell me when to begin. 3. He does not appreciate that the job will take a lot of time. 4. Do you know how to make it work?   5. He is a singer of great promise.   6. Have you discovered where it was made?   7. Ask whether they have any in stock.   8. The book describes what you have to do to make it work again.   9. I don't understand why it won't fit.   10. Will you show me how it opens?

Revision

Exercise 172

Explain the following terms, and check your accuracy by referring to the chapter.

1. dependent clause   2. adjectival equivalent   3. phrase   4. adverbial equivalent   5. apposition   6. noun equivalent.

Exercise 173

Say whether the dependent clauses in the following are adjectival clauses, adverbial clauses or noun clauses, and say what their function is in each sentence.

1. I've put it where it won't get damaged.
2. Show me where it's damaged.
3. The place where it's damaged is not very prominent.
4. The reason that he gave was not very convincing.
5. He claimed that he was under-paid.
6. The paintwork shone when he had finished.
7. Do you remember the time when the marquee blew down?
8. I don't know when he's due back from holiday.
9. Look both ways before you cross the road.
10. The school will be decorated during the week before the holidays end.

Exercise 174

Say whether the italicised groups of words are adjectival equivalents, noun equivalents or adverbial equivalents.

1. *For years* he has been sitting *in the same office*.
2. He writes *with great elegance*.
3. *A photographic skill* derives *in part* from *quickness of reaction*.
4. Fog, *spreading from the Channel*, will cover *the southern part of England* by nightfall.
5. Nelson, *England's naval hero*, is commemorated *by a statue*.

Exercise 175

Expand the words italicised into clauses, and say whether they are adjectival, adverbial or noun clauses.

1. The swimming bath was illuminated by lights *placed below the water-line*.

2. The engineer reported *a leak in the boiler*.
3. It was found *in the deepest part of the lake*.
4. A close examination revealed *numerous faults in the mechanism*.
5. *At the height of the storm,* the race had to be stopped.

12   Kinds of Sentences

We have noticed three kinds of word-groups: the phrase, the clause and the sentence. We must now look at these in greater detail.

1 The phrase

A phrase is a group of words (two words or more) that makes sense but not complete sense. A phrase does not contain a finite verb. A phrase is normally found as part of a larger sentence. There are four types of phrase, but it is not necessary to learn the names of these types as long as their function as phrases is clearly understood.

(*a*)   A phrase may be introduced by a preposition:
> *under* the earth, *beyond* our means, *for* three weeks, *above* suspicion.

A phrase which begins with a preposition is called a *prepositional phrase*.

(*b*)   A phrase may be introduced by an infinitive:
> *To find* the answer, *to open* the discussion, *to bury* the hatchet.

A phrase which begins with an infinitive is called an *infinitive phrase*.

(*c*)   A phrase may be introduced by a participle (past or present) or gerund:

having retired early, *being* a stickler for detail, *folded* neatly.
A phrase which begins with a participle is called a *participial phrase.*

(*d*)   A phrase may be introduced by an adverb:
>   *much* too long, *very* quickly indeed, *quite* heavily.

A phrase which begins with an adverb is called an adverbial phrase, though the other kinds of phrase may be used adverbially.

It is important to note that prepositional, infinitive and participial phrases may go along with subject, object or predicate, but the adverbial phrase is used only with the predicate.

Examples:

(*a*)   prepositional phrases
>   The leader *of the council* was heckled.   (part of the subject)
>   They heckled the leader *of the council.*   (part of direct object)
>   He is a member *of the council.* (complement)
>   They were ejected *from the town hall.*   (part of the predicate, used adverbially)

(*b*)   infinitive phrases
>   *To catch rabbits* is relatively easy.   (used as the subject of *is*)
>   He wants *to catch rabbits.*   (used as object of *wants*)
>   It is a snare *to catch rabbits.*   (part of the complement)
>   He has gone *to catch rabbits.*   (part of the predicate)

(*c*)   participial phrases
>   *Swimming strongly*, he soon reached the shore.   (present participle, used adjectivally as part of subject)
>   *Swimming for such a long period* exhausted him.   (gerund, used as subject of *exhausted*)
>   He keeps the collection *locked away in the bank.*   (past participle, used adjectivally as part of direct object of *keeps*)
>   He regrets *having said that.*   (gerund, direct object of *regrets*)

He has become a man *respected by everyone.* (past participle, part of complement, used adjectivally of *man*)

(*d*) adverbial phrases
Time passed *very quickly indeed.* (describing verb)
It was *exceedingly difficult to understand.* (complement)

Exercise 176

Use the following prepositional phrases in sentences (e.g. the
prepositional phrase *in time* can be incorporated into the sentence
They arrived at the hotel in time to get a drink.).

1. at times   2. with time to spare   3. in former times   4. from
time to time.

Exercise 177

How many prepositional phrases can you form using the word
hand?

Exercise 178

Use the following infinitive phrases in sentences.

1. to turn over a new leaf.   2. to put the cart before the horse.
3. to hit the nail on the head.   4. to travel slowly.   5. to take a
holiday.

Exercise 179

Use the infinitive phrase *to arrive punctually* in sentences as

1. subject of the verb   2. direct object   3. complement.

Exercise 180

Construct sentences including the following participial phrases.

(First re-read Chapter 4, section 13 (b) and (c).)

1. subject of the verb   2. direct object   3. complement.

1. holding their breath   2. feeling their way   3. having finished the meal   4. stuck to the floor.

2   The clause

It has already been seen that a clause is a group of words containing a finite verb, i.e. a subject and a predicate. The clauses we have dealt with so far have been *dependent* clauses, i.e. clauses that do not make complete sense on their own, but contribute to the fuller sense of the sentences of which they form part. In the last chapter, special attention was paid to adjectival clauses, to some adverbial clauses (of place, time and manner), and to one type of noun clause (the noun clause object of a verb). There are many other different types of adverbial and noun clauses, both of which will be dealt with later in this chapter, as will the *main clause*, a type of clause that does make sense on its own.

Exercise 181

Construct sentences using the following as

> (*a*)   noun clause object of a verb
> (*b*)   adverbial clause
> (*c*)   adjectival clause

1. when the tide turns.   2. where it can be found.

Exercise 182

Do graphic analyses of the six sentences you wrote for Exercise 180.

3   The sentence

The third word-group is the sentence, a group of words that can stand on its own, making complete sense. A sentence must always contain at least one finite verb.

For the purposes of explaining the grammatical composition of sentences, it is possible to identify four different kinds of sentence: the simple sentence, the double sentence, the multiple sentence and the complex sentence.

4 The simple sentence

A simple sentence is one which contains only one finite verb:

> An old man sat by the side of the road.

The word *simple* does not refer to the contents of the sentence, nor to its length. It means that it has *one* finite verb.

> An old man, with steel-rimmed spectacles and very dusty clothes, sat by the side of the road, seeming not to notice the carts, trucks and men, women and children, pouring across the pontoon bridge to the other side of the river.

Despite its length, this is a simple sentence because it has one finite verb *sat*, which has the subject *man*. The other verbs, *seeming* and *pouring*, are not finite verbs but participles, i.e. non-finite verbs.

You will remember from Chapter 1 that sentences may take the form of statements, questions, commands and exclamations. All of these are simple sentences if they have only one finite verb. All the sentences quoted as illustrations in Chapter 1 are simple sentences. Look again at Exercises 7 and 9 for examples of simple sentences, both short and long.

A sentence may have a double subject:

> The mule-carts and trucks moved slowly up the steep hill towards the bridge.

The double subject *carts and trucks* consists of two nouns linked by the conjunction *and*, but there is only one finite verb (*moved*) and so the sentence is a simple sentence. Similarly, you may find a sentence with a double object:

> The old man wiped his spectacles and face.

or a pair of adjectives describing a noun, or a pair of adverbs describing a verb. But if there is only one finite verb, the sentence is a simple sentence.

Very often, especially in everyday speech, one does not use

complete sentences. For example, if you pick up the telephone to answer it you might say, 'Hello, Walter Plinge speaking', or if someone asks you the time you might reply, 'Just gone five'. When ordering drinks you might say, 'Two pints of bitter, please', or you might apologise by saying, 'Sorry, my mistake'. you could express all these ideas in complete sentences: 'Hello, this is Walter Plinge speaking', 'The time is just past five o'clock', 'Could I have two pints of bitter, if you please' and 'I am sorry; that was a mistake on my part', but short-hand versions of these and other sentiments are obviously very common in day-to-day conversations. The short versions mean exactly the same as the longer ones.

According to the clearly stated rule, a sentence must contain a finite verb. Statements such as 'Just gone five' and 'Two pints of bitter, please' do not contain finite verbs. None the less, they are merely conveniently abbreviated forms of properly constructed sentences with finite verbs: 'The time *is* just past five o'clock', 'Could I *have* two pints of bitter, please'. The finite verbs are readily 'understood' in the shorter versions, which may therefore be termed *elliptical sentences* ('elliptical' comes from a Greek work meaning 'left out').

Some common words have a similar status as sentence-equivalents. *Please* means *if you please*; *good-bye* means *God be with you*; *yes* and *no* mean *I agree* and *I refuse*. There are many others.

Exercise 183

Express the following as full sentences.

1. Pardon? 2. Sorry 3. No smoking 4. The more the merrier 5. Tickets, please 6. Scotland Yard in New Probe 7. Director Sacked 8. 75p. off 9, Dual Carriageway Ahead 10. What?

5 The double sentence

Consider the sentence

> The taxi drove away and she was left alone.

There are two finite verbs in this sentence: *drove*, of which the subject is *taxi*, and *was*, of which the subject is *she*. The sentence is made up of two clauses, each containing a finite verb, and linked by the conjunction *and*. Neither of the clauses is dependent of the other for its grammatical function; they are both of equal importance, and could in fact have been expressed as two separate short sentences if the author had wished:

> The taxi drove away. She was left alone.

Presumably the writer had good reason for not expressing them in this way: perhaps he thought the effect would have been too jerky and breathless (short sentences are often used to build up excitement); alternatively he may have thought that the two ideas (the taxi driving away, her being left alone) were so closely related that they ought to be connected by *and*.

A sentence of this kind is called a *double sentence* (some grammar books call it a *compound sentence*). A double sentence is really two sentences joined by a conjunction. Once they are joined, they are no longer sentences, of course, but clauses (a clause being part of a longer sentence). In the example quoted above, two simple sentences have been joined into one double sentence consisting of two clauses. Because the clauses make complete sense on their own (*the taxi drove away; she was left alone*), the clauses are called *main clauses*; they do not depend on any other clauses in order to make sense. The notion of main clauses will be looked at more fully later in this chapter.

The two clauses of a double sentence are said to be co-ordinate (of the same rank), and the conjunction that joins them is a co-ordinating conjunction.

If the subject of the second clause is the same as the subject of the first, the second subject is often omitted:

> He preached in every part of England and attracted crowds everywhere.

The subject of *attracted* is *he*, and this is so obvious that there is no need to include a second *he* before *attracted*. The sentence is still a double sentence even if the subject of the second clause is 'understood' as being the same as in the first.

Exercise 184

Link the following pairs of sentences into double sentences.

1. I knocked twice. I received no answer.
2. The policeman held up his hand. The traffic stopped.
3. The policeman held up his hand. The traffic did not stop.
4. The river burst its banks. The river flooded the neighbouring fields.
5. He did not come. His wife did not come.
6. You must hurry. You will be late.

6 The multiple sentence

Just as a double sentence consists of two sentences joined into a single sentence by a conjunction, a multiple sentence consists of three or more such components.

Suppose you wished to express the following three ideas:

      (i) She went into the dining-room.
      (ii) She searched thoroughly.
      (iii) She still could not find it.

You could express yourself in three separate, simple sentences, as listed above. Alternatively you could link them into one single multiple sentence consisting of three main clauses linked by conjunctions:

    She went into the dining-room *and* (she) searched
      thoroughly *but* (she) still could not find it.

Suppose you wished to express three other ideas:

    She sat down. She picked up the newspaper. She began to
      read carefully.

If you decided that you did not wish to use three simple sentences, you might prefer

    She sat down *and* picked up the newspaper *and* began to
      read carefully.

You might think that this was clumsily repetitious, and decide on
 She sat down, picked up the newspaper and began to read
  carefully.
The first *and* has been replaced by a comma, which does the
linking work instead. In its final form, this sentence is still a
multiple sentence even though

 (i) one of the conjunctions has been omitted.
 (ii) the subjects of the finite verbs in the second and third
     main clauses have been omitted because it is quite clear
     that the subject of all three clauses is *she*.

The basic structure remains the same: three main clauses of
equal status, properly linked by conjunctions or by an appropriate substitute (in this case, a comma).

 The three clauses (or more) of multiple sentences are co-
ordinate clauses, and conjunctions that link them are co-ordinate
conjunctions.

Exercise 185

Say whether the following sentences are simple, double or
multiple.

1. The tower is a famous landmark and can be seen for miles
   around.
2. The searchers have been looking for the lost child over a
   wide area of moorland, in the thick woods near the child's
   home, and in pools and mine-shafts.
3. Hearing a cry from a disused barn, one of the search-party
   went to investigate, only to find a solitary sheep.
4. The sailor had brought many presents back from his voyage,
   including some jewellery for his wife, a large wicker basket
   for his mother, and many toys for his children.
5. She felt that something was wrong, but shut the idea from
   her mind, trying hard to concentrate on other things.
6. Hurry up and finish getting ready, or we'll be late.
7. Will you all please sit down and listen carefully?
8. The cyclists streamed past in a sudden flash of colour, turned
   the corner at great speed, and were gone.

Exercise 186

Rewrite the following double sentences as simple sentences.

1. There was a violent thunderstorm and the match was held up.
2. The heat was intense and several spectators fainted.
3. He tried all manner of schemes but they all failed.
4. I was astonished and could not speak.
5. She is a gifted pianist and has many admirers.
6. They were losing heavily at half time, but eventually won, to everyone's surprise.
7. I have become a man and put away childish things.
8. He was dressed unconventionally and people laughed at him.
9. The pumps will have to be repaired or there will be further losses.
10. He did not come, nor did his wife.

7   The complex sentence

Consider the following sentence:

> When he returned home, he spent several hours writing down his thoughts.

There are two finite verbs in this sentence (*returned* and *spent*, both with the subject *he*) and therefore two clauses:

> (i) When he returned home
> (ii) he spent several hours writing down his thoughts

You will notice that one of these clauses makes complete sense, and could in fact stand on its own as a sentence in its own right. That is clause 2. The other clause makes sense but not complete sense; it cannot stand on its own as a complete sentence; it depends for its significance on clause 2. The one that makes complete sense is called the *main clause* (some grammar books prefer *principal clause*). The one that depends on the main clause is a *dependent* (or *subordinate*) clause. In the example quoted, the dependent clause tells us when the action of the verb in the main clause takes place: because it describes a verb it is doing the work of an adverb and is called an adverbial clause of time.

A sentence made up of a main clause and one or more subordinate clauses is called a *complex sentence*.

There are three types of subordinate clauses: adjectival clauses, adverbial clauses, and noun clauses. Reference has been made earlier to these types of clauses, but it is necessary now to examine them in closer detail.

8   The complex sentence: adjectival clauses

We have already dealt with some aspects of the adjectival clause, and some of what follows is therefore revision.

(*a*)   Consider the following sentence:

> He carefully fitted a tiny screw which he took from his pocket.

There are two finite verbs: *fitted*, of which the subject is *He*, and *took*, of which the subject is *he*. There are thus two clauses:

> (i) He carefully fitted a tiny screw
>
> (ii) which he took from his pocket

One of these, the first, is capable of standing on its own as a complete sentence: it is the *main clause*. The other makes sense, but not complete sense: it contributes to the meaning of the whole sentence, and depends on it in order to make that contribution. It is a clause, within a sentence, adding to the meaning of the noun *screw*: it is a dependent or subordinate adjectival clause qualifying *screw*.

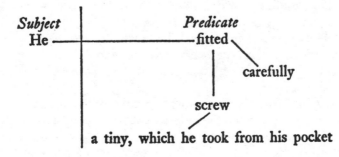

An adjectival clause is a group of words containing a finite verb and describing a noun, pronoun or noun equivalent in the main clause.

Adjectival clauses may be joined to nouns or pronouns in the main clauses by such words as *who, whom, whose, which, that, as, where, when, why*, but in order to identify any clause it is always necessary to ask 'What work is this clause doing?' 'What word (noun, verb, etc.) is this clause describing?' Do not go simply by the word that introduces the clause. Some of the joining words just listed can introduce other sorts of clauses besides adjectival ones.

The word linking an adjectival clause to a main clause may sometimes be omitted. For example

We stayed in a place you won't have heard of.

means

We stayed in a place *that* (or *which*) you won't have heard of.

Despite the lack of the relative pronoun *that* (or *which*), the words *you won't have heard of* are an adjectival clause qualifying *place*. The omission of the relative pronoun (or adjective or adverb) is very common in English.

Exercise 187

Identify the main clauses and subordinate adjectival clauses.

1. He is very careful of his appearance, which is always immaculate.
2. His sister-in-law, who runs a small hotel, has never married.
3. The room to which he was directed was empty.
4. The candidates were assembled in the room where the interview was to take place.
5. He had small hands which he twisted nervously.
6. Can you explain the reason why the fan does not work?
7. She lived alone with her mother, to whom she was very devoted.
8. It dates from the time when the caves were lived in.
9. He is an actor whose talents are not sufficiently appreciated.
10. They had the same trouble as we did.

Exercise 188

Pick out the adjectival clauses in the following.

1. Do you know why he 'phoned?
2. The story he told was hardly credible.
3. The book he is writing is due for completion next month.
4. Gibraltar was the last port they called at.
5. What was the name of the hairdresser you recommended?
6. Put it where the children can't reach it.
7. It was a day when nothing seemed to go right.
8. The leading climber slipped when the party was leaving the summit.

(*b*) Consider these sentences:
    (i) It is an area which is dangerous to shipping.
    (ii) Few ships were in the area, which made a rescue operation difficult to organise.

Both sentences consist of two clauses. The first sentence has a main clause *It is an area* and a subordinate clause *which is dangerous to shipping*; the latter clearly describes the noun *area* and is therefore an adjectival clause.

But what about the second sentence? The two clauses are *Few ships were in the area* and *which made a rescue operation difficult to organise*. The second looks like an adjectival clause introduced, as adjectival clauses often are, by the relative pronoun *which*. But does it describe a noun in the other clause? It does not describe *ships* or *area*. It refers back to the whole of the preceding clause and the meaning is

Few ships were in the area *and this fact* made a rescue operation difficult to organise.

The second clause is not an adjectival clause but a second main clause, co-ordinate with the first. The word *which* in this sentence has a co-ordinating value.

Exercise 189

Say whether the italicised clauses are subordinate adjectival clauses or co-ordinate main clauses.

1. The general, *who was an inspiring leader*, was killed by a stray bullet.
2. The general was killed in the early stages of the battle, *which was a serious blow to the men's morale*.
3. In the early stages of the battle, *which was to last for days*, weather conditions were atrocious.
4. He was out of the country on the day *war broke out*.
5. The car's tyre burst at the first bend, *which marked the end of the race for the world champion*.
6. The injury was not serious, *which was a great relief*.
7. The news, *which was a great relief*, was given us by the hospital.
8. 'Dice' is the plural of 'die', *which is not generally known*.

(*c*)   The adjectival clause should be used with care in the following respects.

  (i) Always place the adjectival clause as close as possible to the word it describes.

Some tinfoil was placed in the sun which was thinly covered with a layer of wax.

It was not, of course, the sun *which was thinly covered with a layer of wax*, but the tinfoil. The adjectival clause should therefore be re-positioned to avoid ambiguity:

Som tinfoil which was thinly covered with a layer of wax was placed in the sun.

  (ii) Problems sometimes occur with the expressions *and who* and *and which*. In the sentence

The passer-by who saw the fire *and who* rescued the trapped children was awarded the George Cross.

there is a main clause

The passer-by . . . was awarded the George Cross

and two adjectival clauses describing the noun *passer-by*:

who saw the fire
who rescued the trapped children.

These two subordinate clauses are joined by *and*. It would have been possible to omit the second relative pronoun *who*:

The passer-by who saw the blaze *and rescued* the trapped children was awarded the George Cross.

This sentence is grammatically correct; so is the original version containing *and who*.

Remembering that the definition of a conjunction is that it links two words, phrases or clauses, consider the sentence

He was a man of quiet courage and purposeful determination *and who* had considerable qualities of leadership.

Here we have two finite verbs (*was*, *had*) and therefore two clauses. The main clause is

He was a man of quiet courage and purposeful determination

and the clause

who had considerable qualities of leadership

is a subordinate adjectival clause describing the noun *man*. The conjunction *and* in *and who* is redundant, because *who* can do the linking work unaided. The first *and* in

quiet courage and purposeful determination

is correctly used to link two phrases, but you cannot join a clause to a phrase by saying

of quiet courage and purposeful determination *and* who . . .

The sentence can be corrected in a number of ways:

He was a man of quiet courage, purposeful determination
and considerable powers of leadership.

He was a man of quiet courage and purposeful determination, who had considerable powers of leadership.

He was a man who had quiet courage and purposeful
determination, and who had considerable qualities of
leadership.

In the last case *and who* is correctly used: two clauses, both beginning with *who*, are linked by *and* as they were in the sentence about the passer-by who was awarded the George Cross.

You must only use *and who* or *and which* if there is a previous clause beginning with *who* or *which*.

(iii) The word *as* may be used as a relative pronoun introducing an adjectival clause when it follows *same* or *such*:

It's the same film as was on last week.

It was such a sight as I've never seen before.

(It would have been possible to use *that* instead of *as* in both of these sentences; *which* would also have been possible in the first.) However, *as* is incorrectly used in

We travelled by the same train as we always travel.

where *as* denotes *by which* (i.e. preposition + relative). It is not possible for *as* to be used as an equivalent for preposition + relative. Correct by

We travelled by the same train by which we always travel.

Exercise 190

Correct the following:

1. She wore jewels in her hair, which her husband had bought her.
2. We made a stop for petrol which lasted about ten minutes.
3. He was given some medicine by a doctor that was distinctly unpleasant.
4. The next exhibit was a fine carriage drawn by two white horses which had red wheels.
5. The Management may refuse admission to anyone it considers proper.
6. He is reading *War and Peace*, a book dealing with Napoleon's invasion of Russia and which is thought by many critics to be a great novel.
7. Children usually like works of fiction and which are full of adventure.
8. She was a woman of great charm and beauty and who was loved by all who knew her.
9. They were treated with a kindness which they never expected and which they fully deserved.
10. It is a house over three hundred years old and which is now sadly in need of renovation.

Exercise 191

Name the adjectival clauses in the following. Correct where necessary.

1. The management made the same offer as they had made previously.

2. The storm was such as no-one had ever experienced before.
3. I was examined by the same doctor as I was operated on.
4. We intend to go to the same hotel as we did last year.
5. The patient is in about the same condition as he was yesterday.

9 The complex sentence: adverbial clauses of time

It has already been seen that, just as a clause may do the work of an adjective in describing a noun, a clause may do the work of an adverb in telling more about a verb.

> The aeroplane landed *late*.
> The aeroplane landed *when the fog lifted*.

The adverb *late* says when the action of the verb happened. It qualifies the verb by telling us the time of the action. It is an adverb of time. The clause *when the fog lifted* does exactly the same work in telling us the time when the action of the verb *landed* in the main clause occurred. It is thus an adverbial clause of time. Because it cannot make full sense on its own, it is a subordinate or dependent clause, describing the verb in the main clause *The aeroplane landed*, which can stand alone making complete sense, and on which the subordinate clause depends.

The subordinate clause is joined to the main clause by *when*, which is therefore a conjunction joining two clauses. (Because it introduces a subordinate clause it is called a *subordinating conjunction*, but this term need not be memorised.)

In graphic analysis, an adverbial clause is placed exactly as if it were an adverb:

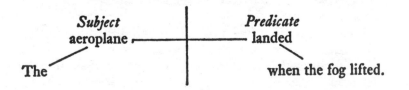

It is not necessary for the main clause to appear first in a sentence: there may be reasons, such as those of emphasis, which make it preferable to place the main clause last:

> Finally, when the fog lifted, the aeroplane landed.

It must not be assumed that words such as *when* always introduce an adverbial clause of time. To identify a clause, it is always necessary to identify its function, and not merely to go by the introductory word. For example:

> The parachutists were standing by the hatch *when the order was given*.

> At the moment *when the order was given*, the parachutists were standing by the hatch.

Although the clause *when the order was given* has exactly the same wording in both sentences, its function is different. In the first sentence it tells us more about the verb *were standing* in the main clause: it says when the action of the verb took place. The clause is therefore an adverbial clause of time. In the second sentence, however, the clause tells us more about the noun *moment*; without the clause, the phrase *at the moment* would mean something entirely different. In this sentence, the clause is an adjectival clause describing the noun *moment*.

Readers interested in the niceties of grammar may care to note that *when* in the first sentence is a (subordinating) conjunction. In the second sentence *when* is a relative adverb. A relative adverb stands for a preposition + a relative pronoun (in this case *at which*), and must always have a preceding noun (or antecedent) to refer to (in this case, *moment*).

Exercise 192

Pick out the adverbial clauses of time.

1. A great deal of litter had to be cleared up after the crowds had left.
2. When the sun is at its hottest, all the streets are deserted.
3. Before he retired he worked in local government.
4. The gardens have remained unchanged since they were first laid out.

5. Hold the ladder steady while I reach into the corner.
6. Stay as long as you like.
7. Latecomers will not be admitted until the first interval.
8. As soon as the final whistle sounded, spectators swarmed on to the pitch.

Exercise 193

State whether the subordinate clauses are adverbial clauses of time or adjectival clauses.

1. One must twist the tourniquet until the bleeding stops.
2. The stallion trembled with excitement when the stable-door was opened.
3. He waited for the moment when the announcement would be made.
4. On the day after the avalanche occurred, first-aid supplies were dropped.
5. It is a school where a lot of science is taught.
6. After the shop opened, a queue formed rapidly.
7. Put it back where you found it.
8. As the flames leapt higher, more and more houses were evacuated.

10   The complex sentence: adverbial clauses of place

Just as it is possible for an adverb to indicate *where* a verb's action takes place
> I've searched *everywhere.*

it is possible for an adverbial clause to do the same work:
> the dog follows him *wherever he goes.*

This clause is an adverbial clause of place, telling *where* the action of the verb *follows* takes place.

Graphically, the two sentences may be shown as follows:

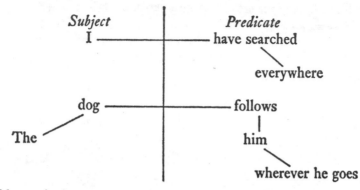

Alternatively we may analyse the second of these as follows:
The dog follows him: Main clause
wherever he goes: Subordinate adverbial clause of place,
    qualifying *follows*.

Exercise 194

Pick out the dependent clauses, and say whether they are adverbial clauses of place or adjectival clauses.

1. Drop me wherever it's convenient.
2. It's best to send it back to the factory where it was made.
3. Where did you live before moving to these parts?
4. I cannot remember where I bought it.
5. You'd better put your knitting where the cat can't get at it.
6. The trawlers are now fishing off Iceland, where the waters are calmer.
7. They have been where no man has been before.
8. Wherever they looked, snow-capped peaks gleamed in the morning sun.

11   The complex sentence: adverbial clauses of manner, comparison or degree

In the sentences
> Fashions change *rapidly*.
> Fashions change *in an unpredictable way*.

the adverb *rapidly* and the adverbial phrase *in an unpredictable way* say how or in what manner fashions change. The work of an adverb of manner can be done by a clause:

The race ended *as all the experts had forecast.*

The subordinate adverbial clause of manner describes the verb *ended* in the main clause by telling us *how* or *in what manner* the ending took place.

A subordinate clause which makes an explicit comparison

In future, people may work shorter hours *than they do now.*

is called an adverb clause of comparison.

A subordinate clause such as the one in

He sings as badly *as he acts.*

does not so much tell us the manner of his singing as the degree of badness, and so may be called an adverb clause of degree, qualifying the adverb *badly* rather than the verb *sings.* A word, phrase or clause that describes an adverb is itself adverbial.

Comparisons including the word *than* are sometimes erroneously or ambiguously composed. For example, what is the difference between the following two sentences?

You love her more than me.

You love her more than I.

The first means

You love her more than (you love) me.

and the second means

You love her more than I (do).

If in doubt as to whether *me* or *I* (or any other nominative or accusative pronoun) is required, complete the sentence mentally by adding the omitted verb, as in the above example.

We often encounter some such expression as

She's a more expert gardener than me.

which should, strictly speaking, be

She's a more expert gardener than I *or* I am.

(The mistake is to assume that *than* is a preposition to be followed by an accusative, whereas it is a conjunction.) Such a 'mistake' is not now taken seriously, but care should always be taken to avoid ambiguity:

You like her more than me.

can mean

> You like her more than (you like) me.

or, more colloquially or 'incorrectly',

> You like her more than I do.

Such an ambiguity should be avoided.

Exercise 195

Pick out the adverbial clauses of manner, comparison or degree.

1. They worked as they had never worked before.
2. Hold the paint-brush as I showed you.
3. He ran as if his life depended on it.
4. He is younger than he appears to be.
5. The loss of life was greater than had at first been feared.
6. They behaved as though nothing had happened.

Exercise 196

Explain the differences between the pairs of sentences

1 *a.* They visit their families more than us.
  b. They visit their families more than we.
2 *a.* I know more about her than he.
  b. I know more about her than him.
3 *a.* I write to her more often than them.
  b. I write to her more often than they.

12 The complex sentence: adverbial clauses of reason or cause

The adverbial clause of time answers the question *when?*
> They worked *until the dawn came.*

The adverbial clause of place answers the question *where?*
> They worked *where they could.*

The adverbial clause of manner answers the question *how?*
> They worked *as they had never worked before.*

The adverbial clause of reason or cause answers the question *why ?*

> They worked *because time was short.*

Adverbial clauses of reason may be introduced by such subordinating conjunctions as *because, since, as, for* and *whereas,* or by phrases such as *seeing that* and *in that.* As always, do not judge by the introductory word, but by the *function* of the subordinate clause.

Exercise 197

Pick out the adverbial clauses of reason.

1. Shipments are being delayed because there is a strike at the ports.
2. As it was late, the meeting was adjourned.
3. As the speech was ending, a member of the audience fainted.
4. Seeing that the ground is uneven, let's pitch the tent elsewhere.
5. They jumped from the windows, since all other means of escape were blocked.
6. Since the last general election, there have been four bye-elections.
7. Since I last saw him he has put on weight.
8. The building proved unsatisfactory in that the corridors were too narrow.

Exercise 198

Construct four sentences using *as* to introduce

1. an adjectival clause
2. an adverbial clause of time
3. an adverbial clause of manner
4. an adverbial clause of reason.

Exercise 199

Construct four sentences using *since* as

1. an adverb
2. part of an adverbial phrase
3. to introduce an adverbial clause of time
4. to introduce an adverbial clause of reason.

Exercise 200

Complete the following with (*a*) an adverbial clause of time, (*b*) an adverbial clause of place, (*c*) an adverbial clause of reason.

1. Men must work . . .
2. The harvest was being gathered . . .
3. The children are enjoying themselves . . .
4. . . . the demolition work was in progress.
5. . . . I shall stay for the night.

13   The complex sentence: adverbial clauses of purpose and result

It is possible for adverbial clauses to indicate the *purpose* of the action described in the main verb, and also the *result* of that action:

He put his weight on the bottom rung of the ladder *so that it would not slip.*   (Purpose)

The windows were so dirty *that it was impossible to see through them.*   (Result)

Just as adverbial clauses of time, place, manner and reason answer the questions *when?*, *where?*, *how?* and *why?* respectively, the adverbial clause of purpose answers the question *for what purpose* (did the action of the verb in the main clause take place)? Words that normally introduce adverbial clauses of purpose include *so, that* and *in order that.*

The negative form of the adverbial clause of purpose may be expressed by using *not*

Turn it off *so that it does not overheat*

or by using the slightly old-fashioned *lest*

> Turn it off *lest is should overheat.*

Nowadays, an infinitive phrase is more common than an adverbial clause of purpose:

> He has come *to read the meter.*

The phrase has the advantage of brevity.

Adverbial clauses of result (or consequence) are normally introduced by *so that* and *such that.*

Exercise 201

Complete the following by supplying suitable adverbial clauses or purpose.

1. All the students studied hard so that . . .
2. The hospital took as X-ray in order that . . .
3. Take care lest . . .
4. A guard is always stationed at the bathing-pool so that . . .
5. We went to bed early . . .

Exercise 202

Pick out the adverbial clauses of result.

1. Mortgage rates are now so high that government intervention is inevitable.
2. House prices are such that first-time buyers cannot afford them.
3. A thick mist came down so that the ferry could not leave.
4. He hurried so that he would not be late.
5. He hurried so as not to be late.
6. The form is so complicated that no-one can understand it.

14 The complex sentence: adverbial clauses of concession and condition

Adverbial clauses of concession are introduced by such subordinating conjunctions as *though, even if, although*:

Although smallpox is rare, vaccination is recommended.

I'll do it *even if it kills me*.

The subordinate clauses express what is conceded or admitted: the sense is that the verb in the main clause takes place granted the circumstances of the subordinate clause.

The concession is sometimes represented by an inversion of the normal order, without a conjunction:

Be it ever so humble, there's no place like home.

The final type of adverbial clause is the clause of condition:

If all goes well, the repairs will be finished by next week.

The subordinate clause qualifies the verb *will be finished*, and defines the *conditions* under which the repairs will be finished by next week. In the following, note the italicised words introducing clauses of condition:

Unless the bridge is strengthened, it will collapse.

The event will cover its costs *provided that* all tickets are sold.

Supposing (that) we leave on Friday, would that be convenient?

Children are admitted *on condition that* they are accompanied by an adult.

In all cases, the subordinate clause indicates the conditions under which the verb in the main clause occurs or may occur.

Consider the sentence

If I were you, I should stay at home.

The subordinate adverbial clause of condition *If I were you* represents a condition that cannot be fulfilled: *I* can never be *you*. It will be seen that the subjunctive *were* is used: *I was* would be incorrect here. In all conditional clauses when the condition cannot be fulfilled or is unlikely to be filled, the subjunctive is used:

If I *were* in charge, things would be done differently.

If he *were* here I'm sure he would agree with me.

The unfulfilled condition may be expressed by means of an inversion:

Had I known, I should have done something about it.

Exercise 203

Construct complex sentences by adding main clauses suitable to the following adverbial clauses of concession.

1. . . . although the sea was calm.
2. . . . though it was still early.
3. Although he reads widely . . .
4. Even if it were possible . . .
5. Efficient as he was . . .

Exercise 204

Pick out the adverbial clauses of condition.

1. Call any time tomorrow, if it's convenient.
2. Call any time tomorrow when it's convenient.
3. We can only succeed if we have their full co-operation.
4. Unless we have their full co-operation, we cannot succeed.
5. Provided we have their full co-operation, we shall succeed.
6. Were we to have their full co-operation, we should succeed.
7. Should he arrive while I'm out, please ask him to wait.
8. We'll come on condition that we're allowed to pay our way.
9. Had I not enquired, we should never have known.
10. If taxes were lowered, unemployment would not fall.
11. Even if taxes were lowered, unemployment would not fall.
12. I'll be hanged if I will.

Exercise 205

Construct four sentences containing subordinate clauses introduced by
so that, two to express purpose and two to express result.

Exercise 206

What is the difference in meaning between the sentences in each of the following pairs?

1 *a.*   If he has witnesses, he will have nothing to be afraid of.
   b.   If he had witnesses, he would have nothing to be afraid of.
2 *a.*   If I can come, I will.
   b.   If I could come, I would.
3 *a.*   If I have a son, I shall be delighted.
   b.   If I had a son, I should be delighted.

Exercise 207

Pick out all the adverbial clauses; state what kind they are and which verbs they describe.

An attempt was made in 1671 by a man named Captain Blood to steal the Crown jewels, which were kept in an iron cage in the Tower of London. As the only guard was over eighty, Blood though it would be an easy task. Disguised as a clergyman, he made frequent visits to the Tower so that he could become friendly with the keeper. He was so successful that he persuaded the keeper to allow his daughter to marry Blood's 'nephew'. When the old man came into the Tower with his daughter for the wedding ceremony, he was seized and bound by four armed men. While one snatched at the crown, the others took possession of the orb and sceptre, but since the latter was too long to be carried inconspicuously, it was sawn into three parts. As they were busily engaged in stowing away the booty, the keeper's son came into the Tower. Although they could have overpowered the youth, the thieves ran out. As they were making their way across St Catherine's Wharf, they were caught. If King Charles had listened to his advisers, he would have punished Blood and his accomplices with stern measures. He did not treat Blood as he deserved or banish him where other enemies of the State had been banished. As Blood had been disappointed in his venture he was given a grant of land in Ireland as a kind of compensation, provided he mended his ways.

15 The complex sentence: noun clauses in the nominative

We have seen that a clause can do the work of an adjective or an adverb. A clause can also do the work of a noun.

Nouns have various functions, in both the subjects and the predicates of sentences. We are here concerned with noun clauses in the nominative case.

(*a*) A noun clause may act as the subject of the verb in the main clause. In the sentence

A bright light appeared in the sky.

the subject is *A bright light*, and the subject-word is the noun *light*, subject of the verb *appeared*.

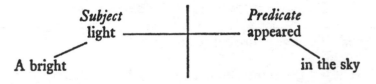

Instead of the subject-word we can have a clause:

What seemed to be a bright light appeared in the sky.

The italicised words are a noun equivalent. They constitute a clause (with the verb *seemed* and the subject *what*). The whole clause acts as subject to the verb *appeared* in the main clause, and the clause is therefore called a noun clause subject:

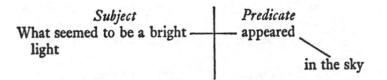

Here are other complex sentences in which the subject of the verb in the main clause is a noun clause subject:

How he failed is a complete mystery.

Who Jack the Ripper was remains unknown.

That he was seriously ill was not widely understood.

(*b*)   A noun clause may be in apposition to the subject:

> The fact *that his licence had been endorsed* counted against
>   him.

The main clause is

> The fact counted against him

and the subordinate clause

> that his licence had been endorsed

is a subordinate noun clause in apposition to the noun *fact*
which is the subject-word of the main clause. You will notice
that the noun clause does not *describe* the noun: it *defines* it. One
could omit the noun *fact* altogether:

> That his licence had been endorsed counted against him.

In this case, the opening clause is a noun clause subject of
counted, but this illustration is intended to show that the noun
clause is doing the same work as the noun *fact*. In

> The fact that his licence had been endorsed . . .

both the noun *fact* and the clause *that his licence had been en-
dorsed* refer to the same thing.

Compare

> The fact that impressed us most was the cleanliness of the
>   place.

Here, the subordinate clause *that impressed us most* does not
define *fact*; it describes it. The word *that* could be replaced by
which. The clause is an adjectival clause.

In

> The fact that his licence had been endorsed counted against
>   him.

the word *that* is a subordinating conjunction. It is, however, a
relative pronoun in

> The fact that impressed us most was the cleanliness of the
>   place.

If you find any difficulty in distinguishing between adjectival
clauses and noun clauses in apposition, try to replace *that* with
some other form of the relative pronoun (e.g. *who*, *whom*, *which*).
If this is possible, the subordinate clause must be adjectival.

(*c*)   A noun clause may be used predicatively, as a complement
of the subject. You will remember that in a sentence such as
National prosperity is their objective, the graphic analysis is

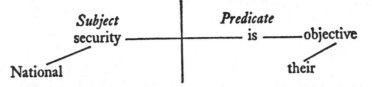

The noun *objective* is used to complete the sense of the verb, because *is* is one of the verbs that may need predicative words in order to complete their sense (see Chapter 10, Section 4, and Chapter 11, section 2c). The noun *objective* is the *complement*. It is possible for a noun clause to do the work of a noun in acting as the complement:

National prosperity is *what everyone wants.*

Here, the clause *what everyone wants* (the finite verb is *wants* and the subject is *everyone*) is doing the same work as was done by the noun (*their*) *objective* in the previous example. The graphic analysis is

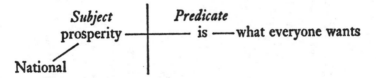

Alternatively, the analysis is

National prosperity is: main clause
what everyone wants: subordinate noun clause comple-
      ment of *is*

In other words, the clause *what everyone wants* is doing the work of a noun in completing the sense of the verb *is* in the main clause. It is a noun clause used predicatively.

Exercise 208

Supply noun clauses to act as subjects to the verbs in the following main clause.

1.   . . . is a considerable achievement.
2.   . . . was no surprise.
3.   . . . puzzled his friends.

4.   . . . remained a secret for years.
5.   . . . cannot be estimated.

Exercise 209

Which of the subordinate clauses are adjectival, and which are noun clauses in apposition?

1.   The announcement that all the passengers were safe was greeted with great relief.
2.   The announcement that was made last evening came as no surprise.
3.   The fact that he was ill is irrelevant.
4.   The fact that we have to face is that funds are inadequate.
5.   The decision that they came to caused much controversy.
6.   I welcome the decision that they came to.
7.   The decision that the building should be demolished is likely to be resisted.
8.   That he will fail is certain.

Exercise 210

Supply noun clauses as complements.

1. The general opinion is . . .   2. The solicitor's advice was . . .
3. Things are seldom . . .   4. The decision was not . . .

16   The complex sentence: noun clauses in the accusative

Just as a noun clause can do the work of a noun or noun equivalent in acting as the subject of a verb, the complement of a verb or in apposition to the subject, a noun clause can act as the object of a verb or preposition or be in apposition to the object.

(*a*)   Noun clauses frequently act as objects to verbs in main clauses. In

The treasurer announced the profit for the year.

the sentence is a simple sentence with one finite verb, *announced*, of which the subject word is *treasurer*. The direct object of the verb is *profit* (and the phrase *for the year* is an adjectival phrase describing the noun *profit*). The sentence could be rephrased:

The treasurer announced *that there had been a profit for the year.*

or

The treasurer announced *what profit there had been for the year.*

The italicised clauses are doing the work of the noun *profit* in the first example. They are therefore called *noun clauses object* of the verb *announced* in the main clause. The analysis can be shown graphically

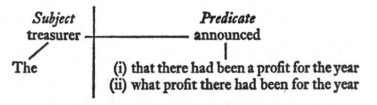

or alternatively

The treasurer announced: main clause

that there had been a profit for the year: subordinate noun clause object of *announced* in main clause.

The linking word *that* is a subordinating conjunction.

The same idea could have been differently expressed:

The treasurer announced, 'There has been a profit for the year.'

Here, there is direct quotation of the actual words used by the treasurer in making his announcement. It looks as if the words in quotation marks are the direct object of the verb *announced* and are thus a noun clause object. This is not so. The quotation marks indicate that the words quoted are separate from the grammatical structure of the sentence beginning *The treasurer announced* . . . It is therefore preferable to regard the quotation as another main clause.

(*b*)   Under certain circumstances, it is possible for a transitive verb (i.e. a verb with a direct object) to need other words to complete the sense. Consider first the sentence

The firm made replacement keys.

where *replacement keys* is the direct object of the verb *made*. Now note the difference between this use of the verb *made* and the following:

His early upbringing made him an avid reader.

Here, the words *an avid reader* are needed to complete the meaning of the verb *made* and are in agreement with *him*, the object of *made*. In this case, *made* is used as a transitive verb of incomplete predication. Instead of the noun *reader*, a noun clause could be used in similar circumstances:

His early upbringing made him *what he was.*

The italicised clause is a noun clause object of the transitive verb of incomplete predication *made*.

(*c*)   We have seen that a noun clause can be in apposition to a noun which is the subject of the verb in the main clause. A noun clause can also be in apposition to a noun which is the object of the verb in the main clause.

They have broken the agreement that all troops should be withdrawn by the end of the year.

Here, the main clause is *They have broken the agreement*, and *agreement* is the object of *have broken*. The subordinate clause *that all troops should be withdrawn by the end of the year* is not an adjectival clause describing *agreement* (remember the hint, given earlier, that adjectival clauses can only begin with *that* when *that* means *which*, *who* or *whom*). It does not describe *agreement*, but defines it: both the noun *agreement* and the clause *that all troops* . . . refer to the same thing. The subordinate clause is therefore a noun clause in apposition to the noun *agreement*, which is the object of the verb *have broken*. Compare

They have broken the agreement *that they made.*

where the subordinate clause is adjectival, describing *agreement*.

(*d*)   You will remember that a preposition is followed by the accusative:

Refreshments are available for *them*.

It is easy to tell when a pronoun is in the accusative, because many pronouns have different forms in the accusative and the nominative. But even when words which do not change their form in the accusative follow a preposition

Refreshments are available for *all visitors.*

they are still said to be in the accusative, as *all visitors* is in this sentence. Accordingly, if a clause is used instead of a pronoun or noun or noun equivalent after a preposition, it is a noun clause in the accusative:

Refreshments are available for *whoever wants them.*

The italicised clause is a noun clause object of the preposition *for.*

Exercise 211

Supply noun clauses to complete the following as objects of the verbs in the given main clauses.

1. The waiter replied that . . .
2. Have you ever realised that . . .
3. Don't tell me that . . .
4. Tell him what . . .
5. Can you explain how . . .
6. No-one seems to know where . . .
7. Detectives have now discovered when . . .
8. Describe . . .

Exercise 212

Supply noun clauses in apposition to the objects in the following sentences. Be careful not to supply adjectival clauses, and if in doubt, remember the test for checking whether a clause beginning with *that* is adjectival or not.

1. The police read out the charge that . . .
2. The government understands the danger that . . .
3. I have a theory that . . .
4. The meeting reached the conclusion that . . .
5. Extremists seem unable to accept the argument that . . .

Exercise 213

Supply noun clauses for the verbs of incomplete predication.

1. Hard work, combined with good luck, has made him . . .
2. You may call me . . .
3. He alone has made the business . . .

Exercise 214

Complete the following by adding noun clauses as objects of the prepositions.

1. Nothing can detract from . . .
2. Can you throw any light on . . .
3. The book was quite different from . . .
4. I wish we could go back to . . .
5. Nothing was said about . . .

Exercise 215

Pick out the noun clauses in the following, stating their kind and function.

1. Five friends decided that they would travel by train to-gether.
2. One of them decided to keep his ticket in his breast-pocket.
3. The fact that the carriage was warm sent him to sleep.
4. What happened next was rather amusing.
5. When they heard that the ticket-collector was approaching, they removed their friend's ticket from his pocket.
6. They awoke the sleeper, who discovered that he had lost his ticket.
    His friends asked him what he was going to do to avoid paying again.
8. What he suggested was the sharing of the cost among all five.
9. The other four were not impressed by what he proposed.

10. One of them had the bright idea that he should hide under the seat.
11. He decided that this was a good idea.
12. That it was also a dirty one soon became apparent.
13. The four friends presented five tickets to the collector, who expressed surprise.
14. His remark was what you might have expected.
15. He asked why there were five tickets for four passengers.
16. The four men then revealed where their friend was travelling.
17. The collector's advice was that the seats were cleaner than the floor.

17 Conclusion

Here are a few miscellaneous points to round off this explanation of sentence-forms.

(*a*) Note that noun clauses, whether subject or object, need not form the subject or object only of verbs in main clauses. They may be found as subordinate clauses to verbs in subordinate clauses.

When I described what had happened, everyone laughed.
Here the main clause is *everyone laughed*. There is a subordinate adverbial clause of time *When I described*, and the verb in this subordinate clause has *what had happened* as its noun clause object.

It is similarly possible for other kinds of subordinate clauses to relate to words in subordinate clauses:

If you see the man who said he would clean the windows,
tell him to call.

There are four finite verbs (*see, said, would clean, tell*) and thus four clauses, of which *tell him to call* is the main clause. *If you see the man* is an adverbial clause of condition describing *tell* in the main clause; *who said* is an adjectival clause describing *man* in the adverbial clause; (*that*) *he would clean the windows* is the noun clause object of *said* in the adjectival clause. Note that the word *that* is often omitted from the beginning of noun clause objects.

(*b*)　It is now possible to complete the definitions of the double sentence and the multiple sentence that were presented in sections 5 and 6 of this chapter. It was stated there that a double sentence is really two sentences joined into one by a co-ordinating conjunction, and that a multiple sentence is more than two sentences joined into a single sentence. It was further explained that, once groups of words capable of standing on their own as sentences have been incorporated into longer double or multiple sentences, these groups of words are clauses, i.e. parts of sentences.

The illustrations of double and multiple sentences given in sections 5 and 6 consisted of simple sentences joined by conjunctions and thus becoming co-ordinate main clauses.

The simple sentences

> The taxi drove away. She was left alone.

were joined by a conjunction to form

> The taxi drove away and she was left alone.

and the analysis of this sentence is that it now comprises two co-ordinate main clauses (i.e. of equal rank) linked by the conjunction *and*. A similarly simple illustration was given to explain the multiple sentence.

Now that we have understood the complex sentence, it can be explained that a double sentence can comprise two complex (or one complex and one simple) sentences linked by a conjunction. One can say

> At first he was surprised. Then he became angry as he realised what was happening.

Here we have a simple sentence, followed by a complex sentence comprising a main clause (*Then he became angry*) and a subordinate clause of time (*as he realised what was happening*). Alternatively we can say

> At first he was surprised, *but* then he became angry as he realised wh t was happening.

We now have one double sentence, of which the analysis is

> At first he was surprised:　main clause

but then he became angry: co-ordinate main clause

as he realised what was happening: subordinate adverbial
clause of time qualifying *became* in co-ordinate main
clause.

In other words, a double sentence is one that has two co-ordinate main clauses. A multiple sentence has more than two. Both types of sentence may have any number of subordinate clauses.

(c)   Remember always that it is not the *form* but the *function* of a clause that determines whether it is a noun clause, an adjectival clause or an adverbial clause. Note the different functions of the clause *when the building was last painted* in

No-one remembers when the building was last painted.
(noun clause object of *remembers*)

Costs were low when the building was last painted.   (sub-
ordainate adverbial clause of time qualifying *were*)

Problems with damp were discovered at the time when the
building was last painted. (subordinate adjectival clause
qualifying *time*)

Revision

Exercise 216

Write out definitions of the following, then check your answers by referring to the appropriate sections.

1. Phrase   2. main clause   3. subordinate clause   4. simple sentence   5. double sentence   6 multiple sentence   7. complex sentence   8. double sentence   9. elliptical sentence   10. adjectival clause   11. adverbial clause of result   12. adverbial clause of condition   13. adverbial clause of concession   14. noun clause   15. noun clause in apposition   16. noun clause complement.

Exercise 217

Each of the following sentences contains a noun clause, an

adjectival clause and an adverbial clause. Identify them, and state their functions.

1. When the war was over, many of the soldiers, who felt that they deserved better, found themselves out of work.
2. Unless there is a last-minute change of heart, the announcement that the factory is to be closed will be made at a news-conference which will be held next Monday.
3. The reason he gave was that demand had fallen since colour-printing had been introduced.
4. How such an accident could happen, especially during a period when special safety measures were in operation, will be carefully investigated, provided that proper co-operation will be available from the Yugoslavian government.

Exercise 218

Construct nine sentences using the following clauses as

(*a*) noun clauses   (*b*) adjectival clauses   (*c*) adverbial clauses
1. where we are going   2. when they left   3. that you eat.

Exercise 219

Construct sentences to illustrate the following.

1. a noun clause subject
2. a noun clause complement
3. an adjectival clause beginning with *why*
4. an adverbial clause of place
5. a noun clause object
6. an adverbial clause of concession
7. an adverbial clause of purpose
8. an adverbial clause of comparison

Exercise 220

Say whether the following are phrases, clauses or sentences. If sentences, say whether they are simple, double, multiple or complex.

1. After the inquest was over.
2. He called and waited, but no answer came.
3. Wait and see.
4. No parking.
5. Into the waste-paper basket.
6. While they were assembling, they stood and chatted.
7. Having achieved their objective, with considerable difficulty and expense of time, the film-crew decided to return to their base, not knowing what to expect after so long as absence.
8. Come when you like.

13 Analysis of Sentences

1 Methods of analysis

So far in this book, sentences have been analysed by the Graphic Analysis method, by which it is possible to see at a glance the construction of a sentence, the subject and its enlargements, the verb and its enlargements, and the object and its enlargements. When we come to deal with longer sentences, we meet more involved constructions. It is recommended that these longer sentences be divided into clauses in a *Tabulated Analysis*. Graphic analysis may be used for the more detailed analysis of simple sentences or of individual clauses, if required.

The process of clause analysis is a division of double, multiple and complex sentences into their component parts: each clause is identified, its kind and function are stated, and its relationship to other clauses is shown.

By understanding clause analysis, we understand how sentences are made up. Many common grammatical errors in speech and writing stem from a failure to understand the basic structures of the English sentence. Correct punctuation is another product of a sound grasp of sentence–construction. If we are familiar with the full range of clause–type and clause–function, the range of our own expression is increased, and our style is improved because we have access to a wider variety of constructions. The purpose of clause analysis is therefore two–fold: to enable us to grasp something of the richness of English language forms, and to enable us to express ourselves with more correctness and variety.

When a sentence is to be analysed into clauses, the following steps should be taken:

(i) Identify all the *finite* verbs. There will be a clause, main or subordinate, for every finite verb.

(ii) Pick out each of the clauses. Remember that sometimes one clause is enclosed within another. In

The competitor who scores fewest points wins.

the clause *who scores fewest points* is enclosed within the main clause *The competitor wins.*

(iii) Look out for conjunctions, relative pronouns, etc. which are often used to link co-ordinate or subordinate clauses.

(iv) Identify the main clause or clauses.

(v) Identify the other clauses. Examine each in turn, and decide on its relationship to the clause to which it is subordinate, which may be the main clause or another subordinate clause.

(vi) Set out the analysis in tabular form (see below).

(vii) State the kind of sentence.

(viii) Use graphic analysis for the more detailed examination of individual clauses if you wish.

2 Complex sentences

Let us now apply the above procedure to a complex sentence.

When he had completed the working model he sent it to numerous manufacturers, who showed little interest.

(i) The finite verbs are *had completed*, *sent* and *showed*, of which the subjects are *he*, *he* and *who* respectively. There are thus three clauses.

(ii) These are

(i) When he had completed the working model

(ii) he sent it to numerous manufacturers

(iii) who showed little interest

(iii) The linking words are *when* (conjunction) and *who* (relative pronoun).

(iv) he sent it to numerous manufacturers: main clause

(v) when he had completed the working model: adverbial clause of time qualifying *sent* in main clause
who showed little interest: adjectival clause qualifying *manufacturers* in main clause

(vi) The tabulated analysis:

	Clause	Kind	Function
A	he sent it to numerous manufacturers	Main Clause	
a¹	when he had completed the working model	Subordinate adverbial clause of time	qualifies verb *sent* in A
a²	who showed little interest	Subordinate adjectival clause	qualifies noun *manufacturers* in A

Note that the capital letter A designates the main clause, which should be placed first, despite its position in the original sentence. Subordinate clauses are designated by small a's, with a raised number to distinguish each clause.

(vii) The sentence is complex: one main clause, two subordinate clauses.

(vii) The individual clauses may be graphically analysed if you wish:

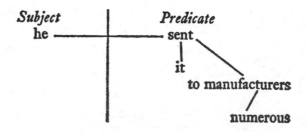

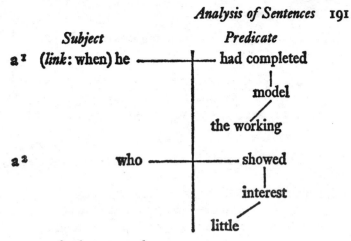

	Subject	*Predicate*
a¹	(*link*: when) he	had completed
		model
		the working
a²	who	showed
		interest
		little

Here are two further examples.

Wherever we went, we discovered that the beaches were crowded.

(i) Finite verbs: *went, discovered, were.*

(ii) Three clauses: wherever we went
we discovered
that the beaches were crowded

(iii) Linking words: *wherever* (conjunction), *that* (conjunction)

(iv) Main clause: we discovered

(v) wherever we went: adverbial clause of place qualifying *discovered* in main clause that the beaches were crowded: noun clause object of *discovered* in main clause.

(vi) The tabulated analysis:

	Clause	*Kind*	*Function*
A	we discovered	Main	
a¹	wherever we went	Subordinate adverbial clause of place	qualifies *discovered* in A
a²	that the beaches were crowded	Subordinate noun clause	object of *discovered* in A

(vii) Detailed graphic analysis if required.

> Although the rioters, who were led by a young fanatic, knew what serious consequences might result from their action, they persisted until troops had to be sent in.

(i) Finite verbs: *were led, knew, might result, persisted, had to be sent.*

(ii) Five clauses: Although the rioters knew
>> who were led by a young fanatic
>> what serious consequences might result from their action
>> they persisted
>> until troops had to be sent in

(iii) Linking words: *although, who, what, until*

(iv) Main clause: they persisted.

(v) Although the rioters knew: adverbial clause of concession qualifying *persisted.*

> who were led by a young fanatic: adjectival clause qualifying *rioters.*

> what serious consequences . . .:   noun clause object of *knew.*

> until troops had to be sent in: adverbial clause of time qualifying *persisted.*

(vi) The tabulated analysis is shown on p. 193.

(vii) Detailed graphic analysis if required.

Exercise 221

Analyse the following complex sentences using the tabulated method. By this stage, it is necessary to use only the steps (i), (ii), (iv)–(vii) of the recommended procedure.

1. Daniel Defoe, who wrote *Journal of the Plague Year*, records an incident which occurred at his brother's warehouse.
2. Whilst he was walking in Swan Alley, he saw a woman coming out of the warehouse with some hats.

	Clause	Kind	Function
A	they persisted	Main	
a¹	although the rioters knew	Subordinate adverbial clause of concession	qualifies *persisted* in A
a²	who were led by a young fanatic	Subordinate adjectival clause	qualifies *rioters* in a¹
a³	what serious consequences might result from their action	Subordinate noun clause	object of *knew* in a¹
a⁴	until troops had to be sent in	Subordinate adverbial clause of time	qualifies *persisted* in A

Type : complex

3. She told him that there were other people inside.
4. The fact that many people were leaving the warehouse with hats made him so suspicious that he went inside.
5. When he had shut the gate behind him, he asked the women what they were doing there.
6. The truth was that they were seizing hats from the warehouse, which apparently had no owner.
7. They thought that they might take possession of them as no-one else was there to claim them.
8. They were unconcerned and quiet as if they had been at a shop.

Exercise 222

Combine the following groups of sentences into single complex sentences.

1. Parliament is opened by the Sovereign at the beginning of each session. The Sovereign outlines the schemes which will be debated by Parliament.

2. Representatives are elected to Parliament by the people. Representatives, who are known as MP's, come from every part of the country.
3. Debates are under the control of the Speaker. He has to be impartial. Debates are sometimes noisy.
4. The policy of the Government is directed by the Prime Minister. He is assisted by the Cabinet. Each member of the Cabinet is responsible for one State Department.

3 Double and multiple sentences

Double sentences have two main clauses of equal importance: one is not grammatically subordinate to the other. Because of this the clauses are called co-ordinating main clauses: neither is dependent on the other in the way that a subordinate clause is dependent on another clause if it is to contribute to the sense of a sentence. Co-ordinate main clauses are linked by conjunctions. A multiple sentence has more than two main clauses. Both types of sentence may additionally contain subordinate clauses.

The steps in the clause analysis of double and multiple sentences are exactly the same as for complex sentences. Here are some examples

(i) We knocked but no-one came.

	Clause	*Kind*	*Function*
A	We knocked	Main	
B	but no-one came	Main	Co-ordinate with A

Type: Double

Note that a new capital letter denotes another main clause.
(ii) They pushed and pulled, but it would not budge.

	Clause	Kind	Function
A	They pushed	Main	
B	and pulled	Main	Co-ordinate with A
C	but it would not budge	Main	Co-ordinate with A and B

Type : Multiple

Note that the subject *they* is omitted before the second finite verb, *pulled*. This does not alter the verb's status as a finite verb.

(iii)   They cleaned and polished it

	Clause	Kind	Function
A	They cleaned (it)	Main	
B	and polished it	Main	Co-ordinate with A

Type : Double

Note that the object *it* is omitted before the first finite verb *cleaned*. This does not alter the verb's status as a finite verb.

(iv)   When the storm was at its height, the gale overturned cars and uprooted trees which had stood for many years.

	Clause	Kind	Function
A	the gale overturned cars	Main	
B	and uprooted trees	Main	Co-ordinate with A
a¹	when the storm was at its height	Adverbial of time	Qualifying *overturned* and *uprooted* in A and B
b¹	which has stood for many years	Adjectival	Qualifying *trees* in B

Type : Double

The sentence is double because there are two main clauses. Had there been only one, the sentence would have been complex. Had there been more than two, it would have been multiple.

Strictly speaking, the clause marked a¹ should be marked a¹b¹, because it qualifies verbs in both A and B equally. This would, however, be cumbersome. Clause b¹ belongs only to B.

A double or multiple sentence may have no subordinate clauses, or one, or more than one.

Exercise 223

Analyse the following in tabular form.

1. The ambulance arrived quickly, but it was too late.
2. They searched and searched, and finally found it.
3. I know and like him, but few others do.
4. The countryside through which we passed was dry and parched, and little farming is possible.
5. After the game was over, the winning team returned to their home town and were given a civic reception, because they had brought home the cup for the first time.
6. An inspector poked his head through the window and informed us that a minor fault had occurred and there would be a delay until it was repaired.

4 Miscellaneous

(*a*) Interjections are not part of the grammatical construction of sentences, and may be omitted in analysis. The same is true of vocatives (i.e. methods of address).

> *Oh dear*, what's gone wrong now?
> *Hello*, who's this?
> Stop it, *Henry*!

(*b*) The word *there* is frequently used:

> What is there for breakfast?
> There's nothing left.
> There are several reasons for the shortage.

Often, the word has a clear grammatical function

> Please put it there.   (adverb)
> There, what did I tell you?   (interjection)
> Fill the glass up to there.   (noun)

but very often (as in the three sentences quoted initially) no such clear grammatical function can be identified; *there* is merely introductory to a verb (often the verb *to be*) that often comes before its subject, as in

There's no explanation.

which is more usual than

No explanation is (*or* exists).

It is simplest to regard *there* as an adverb of place, even though it may now have lost all the force of such an adverb.

(*c*)   Another common usage concerns the pronoun *it* in such sentences as

It was fortunate that we had a map with us.

This sentence could be expressed as

That we had a map with us was fortunate.

so that the *it* is eliminated and *That we had a map with us* is a noun clause subject of *was* in the main clause. However, such a sentence construction would be unusual, almost unidiomatic; the introductory *it* has probably become used in such cases because of a desire not to delay too long the verb in the main clause, which is always the most important part of a sentence.

It is probably best to regard *that we had a map with us* as a noun clause in apposition to *It*.

(*d*)   A non-finite part of the verb may govern a subordinate clause.

They pressed on, hoping *that their luck would change.*

The present participle *hoping* is a verbal adjective, describing the pronoun *They*. Being part of a verb, however, it can have an object, and *that their luck would change* is a noun clause object of the present participle. The tabulated analysis is

	Clause	*Kind*	*Function*
A	They pressed on hoping	Main	
a¹	that their luck would change	Noun Clause	Object of present participle *hoping* in A

Type: Complex

Revision

Exercise 224

Analyse the following in tabular form.

1. He consulted a time-table and found that there was a train which would get him to Crewe before the wedding was due to start.
2. That day a blizzard overtook them with such violence that the leader realised no-one could survive in such fury.
3. No-one could predict how the war would spread, or how long it would last, or how it would end.
4. The boys were so closely alike that no-one could identify them if he tried.
5. It is uncertain how things will end.
6. Despite expectations that it would soon stabilise, the divorce rate is now so high that a Royal Commission is likely to be announced when Parliament resumes.
7. A television director controls the cameras by means of the headphones each cameraman wears, and personally decides which shots he will use.
8. Everyone has some experience of failure, and an honest record of how it feels is the chief merit of this short story, published last week.
9. Two nouns are said to be in apposition when they are similar in meaning and are identical in grammatical function.
10. He was sitting up in bed and rocking from side to side as though he were riding a horse, but at the sight of me his hands dropped from the reins and lay quiet.
11. Refrigerated ships now bring meat from South America that is no dearer than English fresh meat, and it is now worthwhile even to fly foods into Britain, such as early vegetables from the Scillies and the Channel Islands, not just for a millionaire's table at a West End hotel, but for the local public to buy in local markets like Brixton or the North End Road.

12. Shakespeare's theatre did well, but it could not survive on his plays alone, because plays ran only for short periods, the repertory had to be large, and capricious audiences had to be given variety.

13. His state of weakness was such that he was unable to digest any food, he was consumed by fever, and he would have died but for the attention of his friends who rescued him from the excesses into which he had been throwing himself.

14. It is obvious that most of those who smoke do not go on to stronger drugs, and it is ridiculous to pretend that they do.

15. After they had eaten, they climbed where the path led them, past a tethered goat and to a grassy place from which they had a wide view of the harbour and the sea.

16. The invasion was not what it at first appeared to be, be-because the troops treated the inhabitants better than they had been led to expect.

17. They decided to draw lots so that there could be no allegations that unfairness had taken place.

18. What is perhaps even more daunting is that starting to rebuild the city involves re-educating thousands of people in their attitude to property.

19. Although they are clearly prepared to hold out for as long as is necessary, it is inevitable that the rebels must finally lose, because their numbers are few and their supplies of food increasingly low.

20. I have always felt very warmly, even nostalgically, towards the area because I was born there, because I love the people and because I am immensely proud of its folk heritage, particularly of the enterprise of one grandfather who was a prosperous silk merchant until he died at the age of thirty-eight, and of the courage of the other, who walked fourteen miles a day to work until he was well into his sixties.

14 Punctuation and Use of Capitals

1 Introduction

An effective speaker is one who makes his points tellingly, whether he is making a speech, taking part in an interview, talking over the telephone, giving instructions or advice to someone, making a point at a meeting or conference, or simply taking part in a conversation with friends. We have all come across ineffective speakers in these and other circumstances: there is the speaker who gabbles away so quickly that his sentences run into one another, or he breaks off in the middle of a sentence to begin another; there is the ponderous speaker who makes so many pauses, so many um's and ah's, that it is difficult to follow his sense; there is the speaker who uses such long sentences that by the time he has reached the end of one, we have forgotten how it began; there is the speaker with bad habits, who begins every sentence with 'Well', and scatters 'You know' and 'I mean' throughout everything he says, so that the listener becomes so fascinated by the habits that he fails to pay attention to what is said.

The effective user of English uses sentences that are correctly constructed and of an appropriate length. There is a place for short sentences, but if they are used to excess they produce an over-emphatic effect, like a news bulletin or the style of popular newspapers. There is a place for long sentences, but only if the structure is clear and one can be sure that one's hearers or readers can absorb them: we have all had the experience of having to re-read a sentence because we have got lost (usually because of the writer's fault) part way through. Variety is to be cultivated, and it is generally best, when in doubt, to go for the short sentence in preference to the long. The effective speaker uses pauses to group together words that go together: you may have heard a young child taking pride in his newly acquired ability to read, and reading aloud to his parents; usually, at this early stage, he reads all the words on the page with the same emphasis, as if they were a list; he has not yet acquired the ability to phrase the words into groups, and transmit the phrasing to the hearer by the rise and fall of voice, and by the natural use of pauses. In other words, he completely ignores the punctuation.

When talking, we instinctively use pauses, some very slight, some longer, to group words into ideas. We use other devices: a slight rise in the voice at the end of a question, a slight fall at the end of a sentence; we also use different tones of voice to suit different moods, or as a deliberate means of avoiding monotony – dull delivery at an unvaried level, irrespective of what we are saying, is another mark of the very poor speaker. We may emphasise key words or phrases with the voice, or by pausing before or after them. Gestures or facial expressions may also play a part in communicating what we have to say.

In writing, however, we are more limited. We have three aids available to us: the choice of the appropriate word; the choice of the appropriate order of words; the choice of the appropriate punctuation. Of these three, the last is the least important, and no manner of punctuation will help if our choice of words and their arrangement are such as to leave our meaning obscure. Of course punctuation is important: there is a substantial difference, if we may quote the old schoolboy howler, between

Charles I walked and talked half an hour after his head was cut off.

and

Charles I walked and talked. Half an hour after, his head was cut off.

There are many occasions when the insertion of a piece of punctuation will make the difference between sense and non-sense, clarity and obscurity. But the first concern of the good and careful writer is to select the most appropriate words in the most effective order.

Punctuation is the means by which a writer indicates the intended grouping of his words. It is, roughly speaking, the equivalent of pauses in speech – not those heavy pauses used for special emphasis, but those almost imperceptible pauses we use naturally, often without realising what we are doing.

Punctuation should not be regarded as a set code of rules; there are some rules that must be learnt and observed, but there is also a great deal of room for flexibility. Punctuation should rather be looked on as a means of ensuring that a passage is divided in such a way that the meaning of the various parts and of the whole is clear and unambiguous. Common sense is more important than rules. Punctuation exists to help one's reader understand. And it is best to try to write so that the reader will need the minimum of help from your use of punctuation. A very useful working principle is that you should try to make your meaning clear without depending too much on punctuation.

2　The full stop

The full stop (.) is used at the end of a sentence, and each new sentence begins with a capital letter (see below). A question mark or an exclamation mark, both of which are dealt with later in this chapter, may be used instead of a full stop where appropriate.

The full stop (sometimes called *the period*) is also used to indicate an abbreviation. An abbreviation may be

(*a*)　a shortened name: *S. N. P. Brackenden*

(*b*)　a shortened title: *The Revd. S. N. P. Brackenden, H.M. Government*

(*c*)　initial letters standing instead of words: *U.S.A., M.A., R.A.F., M.P.*

(*d*)　any shortened word: *Feb.* 3, *St. Jude*

It is now common, however, to omit full stops after *Mr*, *Mrs* and *Dr*, and also after well-known abbreviations that are used almost as frequently as the words they signify, such as the ones in (*c*) above. Many newspapers, in fact, now omit all full stops from abbreviations.

If an abbreviation ends a sentence, one full stop is sufficient to signify both the abbreviation and the end of the sentence.

Exercise 225

How many abbreviations can you add to the list in (*c*) above?

Exercise 226

Insert full stops where needed.

Swift defined a good style as the use of proper words in proper places the proper places will vary considerably according to degrees of emphasis usage has left many parts of the sentence relatively free and these we can vary to suit our purpose the poet Coleridge laid much stress on the importance of word order he defined poetry as 'the best words in the best order' he asserted that there is in the words of the greatest poets 'a reason not only for every word but for the position of every word' in the well-ordered sentence the hearer or the reader will receive no jolt or check Herbert Spencer observed that things which are to be thought of together must be mentioned as closely as possible together naturally we place together such words as are more closely associated in meaning we say *a big brown dog* rather than *a brown big dog*, *a handsome young man* and not *a young handsome man*, and *a kind old gardener*, not *an old kind gardener* so too we place together those phrases which are most closely associated in our minds 'Delighted to make your acquaintance' we say upon being introduced, not, as in German, 'Delighted your acquaintance to make'.

(Simeon Potter: Adapted.)

3   The comma

Perhaps the most common error in the writing of English is to use a comma in order to separate sentences. A comma *cannot* be so used, and the following are incorrect:

I am returning the electricity bill you sent me, it is incorrect.

We arrived here yesterday, the weather is perfect.

None of the photographs came out, the camera was broken.

Full stops (or their equivalent, as described in later sections) should have been used in place of commas, or the sentences should have been linked in some way, e.g. by inserting *because* before *it* in the first sentence.

The comma is used

(*a*)   to mark off a phrase or clause, or occasionally a word, when the sense demands a slight pause:

Women are, for the most part, more interested in clothes than men are.

The British Constitution, as everyone knows, has been shaped by retaining old forms and putting them to new uses.

However, many writers prefer complexity to simplicity.

(*b*)   to separate words (occasionally phrases or clauses) in a list:

The guests included ambassadors, envoys, consuls and other representatives of the diplomatic service.

A comma is unnecessary before *and* at the end of a list, but it is not incorrect and may be needed for emphasis or to avoid ambiguity.

(*c*)   when an inversion of the normal order is used for emphasis:

He surveyed the damage grimly.

but

Grimly, he surveyed the damage.

(*d*)   before a direct quotation:

An anonymous diplomat once wrote, 'If you take trouble

in the use of words you are bound to clarify the thought you wish to convey.'

(*e*)   on any occasion where its presence helps the reader. But remember what has been said about the importance of words and word order, rather than of punctuation, as a means of expressing what you have to say. If you write

> She arrived with her husband and two cats in a basket.

you may decide that you have committed an unfortunate ambiguity, and decide to clarify by adding a comma:

> She arrived with her husband, and two cats in a basket.

Better to have avoided the ambiguity in the first place by a more careful choice of words:

> She arrived with her husband and with two cats in a basket.

Another example:

> It can be mended perhaps with a screwdriver.

may mean

> It can be mended, perhaps with a screwdriver.

(which means that it can be mended), or the meaning may be

> It can be mended perhaps, with a screwdriver.

(which means that there is some doubt about whether it can be mended). There is no ambiguity in

> It can perhaps be mended with a screwdriver.

or

> It can be mended if you use a screwdriver.

Exercise 227

Write out the following, inserting commas and full stops. remember that to insert a comma where it is not required is as incorrect as to omit one where it is required.

(*a*)   Sir Boyle Roche who is credited with some incredible statements is reported to have said 'Single misfortunes never come alone and the greatest misfortune is generally followed by a much greater one'.

(*b*)   Since the war of 1939–45 and partly because of it there has arisen a Do-It-Yourself cult affecting not only the practicalities of life but also its embellishments and enhancements and consolations: music and the arts literature and the drama all show an undermining by the levelling process those for whom 'anything goes' have yet to learn that ultimately for them nothing goes lacking a worth-while ambition a compulsive aspiration a genuine integrity they are easily satisfied with mediocrity for them the speech of an illiterate is preferable to that of an educated cultured person subtlety and suppleness distinction and variety eloquence and ease clarity of phrasing and perspicacity of sentence all these are suspect for they imply superiority of mind and spirit no wonder mediocrity flourishes in literature and indeed at all levels of writing for its own vehicle language has been slowed down by the dull and the indifferent anyone who believes in civilisation must find it difficult to approve and impossible to abet one of the surest means of destroying it to degrade language is finally to degrade civilisation

(*Eric Partridge: Adapted*)

4 The colon

The colon (:) is stronger than the comma or semi-colon (see below) but weaker than the full stop. Some writers do without it altogether, but it has several valuable uses:

(*a*) at the end of a main clause when what follows is an amplification:

> The system has three drawbacks: it is too expensive, it takes too much time, and no-one understands it.

A full stop would have been possible after *drawback*, but what follows is sufficiently closely linked to *The system has three drawbacks* to justify the less sharp separation provided by the colon. A comma would have been wrong, however. Why?

(*b*) to introduce a quotation, as the colon does after *amplification* in the previous paragraph, and as it is used frequently in similar circumstances throughout this book.

(*c*) to introduce a list:

> Dickens wrote a number of important novels: *Bleak House, Oliver Twist, David Copperfield* and *Hard Times*.

A comma would not have been strong enough here, though one could have said

> Dickens wrote a number of important novels, including
> *Bleak House, Oliver Twist* . . . .

where the sense requires no pause, and therefore no punctuation, before *Bleak House.*

5   The semi-colon

Like the colon, and unlike the comma, the semi-colon is a stop rather than a pause, but not as complete or heavy a stop as the full stop. The semi-colon is used to break up long sentences; it relates clauses or sentences which have too strong a relationship to be separated by full stops. What follows and precedes a semi-colon must be a grammatically complete sentence. In other words, the semi-colon is an alternative to the full stop when the writer wishes to link, rather than separate, what follows and what has preceded. A semi-colon should not be used to mark off mere phrases and subordinate clauses (for which a comma suffices); it should mark off sentence-equivalents.

> The crematorium charges are not excessive; they have not
> risen for ten years.

Here, the semi-colon links two simple sentences. A full stop could have been used; alternatively, the sentences could have been linked to a conjunction such as *and.* It would not have been incorrect to use a colon on the grounds that the second statement amplifies or explains the first. The semi-colon is correctly used to link two sentences which have a common topic.

> The story is told of a man who had been suffering from
> insomnia for many years; no-one could find a cure.
> Finally, his friends hit upon a plan which succeeded
> perfectly: he was given a job as a night-watchman, told
> to stay awake at all costs, and was found asleep within
> the hour.

The semi-colon is used to link the first (complex) sentence and the following (simple) one which is closely related to it. The colon after *succeeded perfectly* indicates that the nature of the success is about to be described. Commas mark off the final three clauses; all of them have the same subject (*he*) and the commas provide the link.

Exercise 228

Punctuate the following. Each one is a single sentence.

1.   Many English river-names are Celtic Avon Severn Thames Trent and Wye
2.   The subjects of the play are love marriage separation and divorce
3.   All was peaceful in the park ducks waddled lovers strolled children played old men slept and a few rowers plied their oars lazily
4.   The company has been making bricks for a hundred years its expertise is thus very considerable
5.   There was a sharp frost in the air it cut the nose and lungs you could feel your eyes water in the darkness

6   The question mark and exclamation mark

(*a*)   The question mark (?) is used at the end of a sentence when a direct question is being asked; a direct question is one in which the words are phrased as an actual question:

What will they think of next?

Has anyone a match, please?

Can you tell me where the nearest telephone-box is?

Single words are sometimes used as questions:

How? When? Where? Who? Why?

Note the differences between the direct questions above and

I wonder what they will think of next.

I asked if anyone had a match.

I enquired where the nearest telephone-box was.

These are not direct questions, because they do not consist of the actual words used when asking the questions. These sentences, therefore, should not have question marks.

(*b*) The exclamation mark (!) is used to indicate a surprised tone of voice, and to punctuate exclamations (see Chapter 1).

Good heavens! We've won!

Do not use exclamation marks excessively, certainly not in formal writing. There is room for them in letters to friends, and in works of fiction, provided that one does not lapse into the habit, frequently found in children's comics, of using them extravagantly:

Wow!!! What?!

In this connexion, a word should be said about the use of underlining. There is a strong temptation to underline a word or phrase for emphasis, perhaps following the royal precedent of Queen Victoria, who in her letters used underlining extensively whenever she felt strongly about something – which was very often. Underlining for emphasis can become a habit; if over-used it merely suggests petulance or high blood-pressure. Used sparingly, it can draw urgent attention to something by its very unexpectedness, but the correct choice and arrangement of words are the best means of being emphatic.

7 The dash

The dash (–) is often too carelessly used in English instead of the comma – and often instead of most other punctuation as well.

Its correct uses are

(*a*) to introduce and conclude an expression (phrase, clause or sentence) introduced into a sentence by way of explanation or comment:

The ghost – so local rumour has it – walks the moors
between Okehampton and Tavistock.

Brackets are sometimes used as an alternative, when a writer wants to slip something in unobtrusively without disturbing his flow, and uses brackets to suggest that the words within brackets are subordinate to the main sense of what he is saying:

A number of defensive walls are linked together to form

the Great Wall of China (the only man-made object
visible from the moon) after the country was unified.

Brackets (sometimes called *a parenthesis*) could have been
replaced by dashes or commas here, though commas would
have brought a rather irrelevant piece of information too strongly
into the main sense of the sentence.

(*b*)   towards the end of a sentence, indicating an anticipatory
pause before a conclusion, explanation or surprise:

The book is what every publisher dreams of – a best-
seller.

(*c*)   at the end of a sentence which is left uncompleted. This
device is often found in works of fiction when a speaker is
interrupted by another speaker or by something that happens:

'If you can't trust me – '
'It's not that I can't trust you. It's just that – '
The argument was interrupted by a shout from outside.

Some writers prefer three dots (. . .), however, in such circumstances.

(*d*)   after a colon, to introduce a quotation or list (:–). This use
is now seldom found, because the colon can do the work unaided.

Avoid over-use of the dash, especially as a parenthesis. Too
many interruptions to the flow of sentences can irritate the
reader; parentheses can often be worked into the main structure
of sentences with a little forethought and without resort to
dashes and brackets. The dash has legitimate functions, as we
have seen, but it offers temptations, especially the temptation
to launch into a sentence without thinking what one is going to
say, secure in the knowledge that afterthoughts can always be
stuck in with the help of dashes.

8   Quotation marks

Quotation marks ('. . .'), sometimes called *inverted commas*, are
used to denote that a speaker's or writer's actual words are being
used:

'That's true,' said Bernard.

The Prime Minister said, 'Prospects are good.'

There is no unanimous agreement about the placing of punctuation, but the above examples show widespread practice. Note that *That's true* is a whole sentence, but a comma follows it; if the words had been a question or an exclamation, a question mark or exclamation mark would have been correct. Sometimes a direct quotation is interrupted by *he said* or some similar expression; note the punctuation in

'She's bought a trampoline,' said Betty, 'so that she can practise every day!'

'Betty's not joking,' said Eva. 'What's more, do you know that she keeps the trampoline in the greenhouse?'

There is a comma after *Betty* because the second part of the quotation continues the sentence begun in the first part. There is a full stop after Eva, however, because the quotation continues with a new sentence. This explains the small *s* of *so* in the first quotation and the capital *W* of *What's* in the second. Note too that it is customary to begin a new paragraph before and after each speech.

The words within inverted commas in the above illustration are called *direct speech*.

Should it be necessary to use a quotation within a quotation, double inverted commas ("...") may be used.

Inverted commas are usually used to punctuate the title of a book, play, film, etc.:

It's many years since I read 'Wuthering Heights'.

9   The apostrophe

The use of the apostrophe (') to indicate possession has already been described in Chapter 2.

The apostrophe is also used to indicate a letter or letters omitted:

don't (do not), shan't (shall not), it's (it is), won't (will not), can't (cannot), I'll (I will)

10   Capital letters

These should be used for

(*a*)   the beginning of every sentence,

(*b*)   the beginning of sentences quoted in inverted commas, as described in section 8,

(*c*)   the beginning of each line of poetry, though much modern poetry does not follow this convention,

(*d*)   proper nouns (see Chapter 2),

Rome, Napoleon, Parliament

and some adjectives formed from some of them,

Roman, Napoleonic

but not all,

He hopes for a parliamentary career.

(*e*)   names of deities:

God, Buddha, Allah

(*f*)   the important words in titles of books, plays, etc.

(*g*)   days of the week, months of the year and special festivals or events:

Sunday, December, Easter, the Trooping of the Colour.

(*h*)   the personal pronoun *I*, but not *me*. Pronouns referring to God are given capital letters in Scripture, theological works, etc.

(*i*)   the poetical device known as *personification*, when abstractions are referred to as people:

To that high capital, where kingly Death
Keeps his pale court in beauty and decay,
He came.

Exercise 229

Insert the appropriate punctuation.

1.   Would you please pass the salt and pepper.
2.   What a strange-looking building

3. They phoned to ask if we could help
4. It wont cost much to replace or so he says
5. Youll never guess what the price is £17
6. The guide-book a handsomely produced volume incidentally describes the library ceiling as the finest in Europe
7. He doesnt understand why it wont start
8. I met a young american in oxford street on monday he told me hed seen all the productions of the royal shakespeare company since easter and liked coriolanus best

Revision

Exercise 230

Show how the meaning of the following may be altered by a change in the punctuation.

1. Wanted – a daily help to wash iron, and clean.
2. 'The foreman,' said the manager, 'does not know his job.'
3. A few miles on the path is much worse.
4. The policeman says the burglar is the bane of his life.

Exercise 231

Commas are incorrectly used to join the following pairs of sentences. Rewrite correctly.

1. Please write soon, we miss you.
2. The cinema is comfortable, the seats are expensive.
3. He is tired, he has been working hard.
4. No thank you, I don't smoke.
5. I am sorry not to have written sooner, I have now been able to check our records.
6. I am returning to you the meat-thermometer, it is not the one I ordered.

Exercise 232

Read the following and satisfy yourself that you can understand why the writer used the punctuation he did.

(*a*)   It is wise therefore not to begin to write, or to dictate, until you are quite certain what you want to say. That sounds elementary, but the elementary things are often the most likely to be neglected. Some, it is true, can never be sure of clarifying their thoughts except by trying to put them on paper. If you are one of these, never be content with your first draft; always revise it; and you will find that practice, though it may not make perfect, will greatly improve your efficiency.

(Ernest Gowers and Bruce Fraser)

(*b*)   Mother always left until the last a fat letter, addressed in large, firm, well-rounded handwriting, which was the monthly instalment from Great-aunt Hermione. Her letters invariably created an indignant uproar among the family, so we all put aside our mail and concentrated when Mother, with a sigh of resignation, unfurled the twenty-odd pages, settled herself comfortably and began to read.

'She says that the doctors don't hold out much hope for her,' observed Mother.

'They haven't held out any hope for her for the last forty years,' said Larry, 'and she's still as strong as an ox.'

'She says she always thought it a little peculiar of us, rushing off to Greece like that, but they've just had a bad winter and she thinks that perhaps it was wise of us to choose such a salubrious climate.'

'Salubrious! What a word to use!'

'Oh, heavens! . . . oh, no . . . oh, Lord! . . .'

'What's the matter?'

'She says she wants to come and stay . . . the doctors have advised a warm climate!'

'No, I refuse! I couldn't bear it,' shouted Larry, leaping to his feet. 'It's bad enough being shown Lugaretzia's gums every morning, without having Great-aunt Hermione dying by inches all over the place. You'll have to put her off, Mother . . . tell her there's no room.'

'But I can't, dear; I told her in the last letter what a big villa we had.'

'She's probably forgotten,' said Leslie hopefully.

'She hasn't. She mentions it her . . . where is it? . . . oh yes, here you are: "As you now seem able to afford such an extensive establishment, I am sure, Louie dear, that you would not begrudge a small corner to an old woman who has not much longer to live." There you are! What on earth can we *do*?'

'Write and tell her we've got an epidemic of smallpox raging out here, and send her a photo of Margo's acne,' suggested Larry.

(Gerald Durrell: Adapted)

Exercise 233

Punctuate the following.

Ride into the town said the squire and see if theres a letter for me yes sir said Andy do you know where to go to the town sir yes but do you know where to go in the town no sir then why dont you ask said the squire havent I told you always to ask if you dont know something Andy paused yes sir he finally said then why didnt you ask because I didn't want to be any trouble the squire couldnt help laughing at Andys excuse for remaining in ignorance well he continued you must go to the post-office

(Samuel Lover: Adapted)

Exercise 234

Write out the answers to the following questions, then check the accuracy of what you have written by referring to the chapter.

(*a*)   How many different types of abbreviation can you think of?
(*b*)   What are commas used for?
(*c*)   Explain the difference between the uses of the colon and the semi-colon.
(*d*)   What are the uses of the dash?
(*e*)   Write out an explanation of the way in which inverted commas are normally used to punctuate direct speech. Refer to Exercise 231 if necessary.
(*f*)   How many uses of capital letters can you remember?

15   Key to Exercises

(If an exercise is such that many answers are possible, no reference will be made to it in this Key.)

Exercise 1

1. sentence   2. sentence   3. not a sentence   4. sentence   5. not a sentence   6. not a sentence   7. sentence   8. sentence   9. not a sentence   10. not a sentence

Exercise 2

(Many answers are possible: the following are merely examples.)
1. The taxi is parked further along the road.
2. She ordered five pints of milk for the weekend.
3. The house, together with all its contents, is to be auctioned.
4. Constructed in the early part of the sixteenth century, the palace was restored in 1853.
5. Only a very few competitors finished the race.

Exercise 3

1. . . . stop. Two . . . road. We . . . talk. He . . . sad. When . . . hand. As . . . windows. Underneath . . . speed. That . . .
2. . . . escape. A wave . . . exertion. It . . . us. With . . . it. He . . . us. I . . .

Exercise 4

1. request   2. exclamation   3. command/request   4. statement   5. question   6. command   7. exclamation   8. question   9. statement   10. statement

Exercise 6

1. An ambulance 2. You 3. his voice 4. Wind and rain 5. The weather-forecast 6. news 7. The rapidly falling birth-rate (*or simply* birth-rate) 8. The play

Exercise 7

The subjects are given: the rest of the sentences constitute the predicate.

1. The subject	2. They
3. I	4. The only way to learn how to spell correctly
5. anyone	6. you
7. Who	8. he
9. You (understood)	10. You (understood)
11. that	12. she
13. It	14. You (understood)
15. What	

Exercise 8

1. sentence: statement
2. phrase
3. sentence: command
4. phrase
5. sentence: question
6. sentence: command/request
7. phrase
8. sentence: exclamation

Exercise 9

1. You (understood)
2. the people from his native village
3. All the words except the final two
4. nobody
5. It

Exercise 10

1. family, fathers, mothers, uncles, aunts, brothers, sisters, cousins, concern, provision, food, shelter, member, family, house, brush, cultivation, woman, fields, hunter, antelope, wife, children, relatives, times, shortage, relative, help.

2. girl, interest, deal, rate, moment, experience, faintness, nausea, feeling, sort, place, room, Durward, Peggy.
3. man, Blackheath, set, teeth, start, Lord, heart. (For *myself*, see Chapter 6.)
4. statement, week's, edition, Mr. A. B. Smith, defective, Police Force, Mr Smith, detective, Police Farce.

Exercise 11

1. bones (common), structure (common), sentence (common), thing (common), years (common), schoolfellows (common), prizes (common), distinction (abstract), poetry (common), epigrams (common), English (proper), living (common), way (common), disadvantage (abstract), favour (abstract), boys (common), English (proper), all (common), English (proper), ones (common), Latin (proper), honour (abstract), Greek (proper), treat (abstract), thing (common), English (proper).
2. hill (common), face (common), moon (common), treetops (common), friendliness (abstract), net (collective), elm-boughs (common), head (common), clusters (common), tufts (common), face (common), company (abstract), touch (common), gentleness (abstract), trees (common), wood (common), sympathy (abstract).

Exercise 12

1. men (the others are collective nouns)
2. tears (the others are abstract nouns)
3. peace (the others are common nouns)
4. loch (the others are proper nouns – though Loch Lomond would have been proper)

Exercise 13

flock, herd, pack, swarm, pride, gaggle, litter, school, staff, choir, orchestra, library, range, shrubbery

Exercise 14

selfishness, caution, politeness, modesty, scarcity, cowardice, guilt, cruelty, bravery, destruction, obedience, choice, temptation, deduction.

Exercise 15

valleys, victories, businesses, wives, armies, cargoes, rushes, chimneys, loaves, watches, lives, sixties, dishes, potatoes, hoaxes, windows, buses, essays, brasses, cliffs, teaspoonfuls, passers-by, bases.

Exercise 16

1. a man's reach   2. a boy's best friend   3. the lions' den   4. men's achievements   5. women's clothes   6. the box's lid   7. the dress's sleeves   8. the dresses' cost

Exercise 17

1. The boys' possessions   2. The children's hobbies   3. The countries' exports   4. Men's aspirations   5. the sheep's safety (no change: *sheep* is the same in singular and plural)   6. Women's place   7. The teams' results   8. The armies' exercises

Exercise 18

1. principal   2. cast   3. chords   4. allusions   5. serial   6. suit   7. surplice   8. effect   9. lightning   10. mail (though *male* is possible if *sort out* is used in its sense of *assault*!)

Exercise 19

1. The next train/is due in twenty minutes.
2. (You)/come into the garden.
3. What/ can be more enjoyable than a long swim on a hot summer's day?
4. We/ shall have another attempt?
5. I/ can actually write my name in the dust on the table.
6. You/ must be joking.
7. He/ did say what?
8. The next opportunity for promotion/ will not occur until next year.

Exercise 20

monkeys, ponies, women, cod, libraries, sheaves, contraltos, marches, waltzes, mottoes, analyses, roofs, memoranda or -dums, on-lookers, ring-side seats, beliefs, thieves, loaves, aquaria, premiums, handkerchiefs, buses, criteria, themselves, commanders-in-chief.

Exercise 21
See section 3

Exercise 22
Refer to a dictionary.

Exercise 23
nun, spinster, lady, widow, duck, masseuse, student, duchess

Exercise 24
wisdom, depth, excitement, confidence, delicacy, rotation, adjustment, capability, eagerness, disobedience

Exercise 25
(There are, of course, alternatives to the following.)
success, adversity; weariness, energy; vigour, weakness; kindness, meanness; tenderness, roughness; bravery, cowardice; satisfaction, discontent; dullness, interest; concord, discord; condolence, callousness.

Exercise 26
frogs', chefs', drivers', England's, France's.

Exercise 27
observation (common), feeling (common), presence (common), beings (common), animals (common), source (common), spider (common), eyes (common), set (collective), masks (common), eyes (common), direction (common), care (abstract), beauty (abstract), design (abstract), Buddhas (proper), objects (common), while (abstract).

Exercise 29
huge, great, massive, wide, mighty, fifty, thick, dark, hideous, black, fierce.

Exercise 32
notorious, their, own, long, endless, each, much, these, great, many, neighbouring, his, own (= own nest), more, another, rascally, few, uninterested, nearest, What, her, own, her, very, his, recent, thieving, another.

Exercise 33
kinder, kindest; more, most benevolent; more, most loving; better, best; purer, purest; holier, holiest; more, most innocent; more, most careless; harder, hardest; more, most cruel (or crueller, cruellest); more, most evil; worse, worst; smaller, smallest; less, least; tinier, tiniest; later, latest; farther, farthest; sillier, silliest; gayer, gayest (or more, most gay), outer; outermost; livelier, liveliest.

Exercise 34
1. than all the other members
2. now higher than *or* omit 'before'
3. omit 'others'
4. omit 'before'
5. omit 'other'
6. the better of the two
7. Both *more preferable* and *preferable than* are wrong. Rephrase: Attack was preferable to withdrawal.
8. greater
9. omit 'very'
10. The sentence is correct, because *almost unique* does not suggest a degree of uniqueness (as *very* does in the previous example). The sentence means that the ceiling is not unique, but nearly so: this is a degree of closeness to the state of uniqueness, not a degree of uniqueness.
11. These kinds.
12. those sorts, *or* that sort of flower.

Exercise 36
1. pointed   2. irreparable   3. unanimous decision   4. credulous
5. initial success   6. prompt   7. submarine life   8. inflammable

Exercise 37
1. in the distance   2. with ginger hair   3. easily taken in
4. without cares   5. beyond belief

Exercise 38
1. less   2. fewer   3. fewer   4. fewer   5. less

Exercise 41
Dutch, Norwegian, Spanish, Swiss, Swedish, Cuban, Peruvian, Parisian, Neopolitan, Viennese, Christian, Buddhist, Caesarean, Napoleonic, Shakespearean, Shavian.

Exercise 42
eventful, homely, talkative, momentous, moody, demonic (*or* demoniacal), serpentine, burdensome, critical, controllable, real, god-like (*or* godly)

Exercise 44
(Several alternatives are possible.)
ignorant, lively, evil, idle, friendly, permanent

Exercise 45
1. fewer   2. types   3. cheaper   4. uninterested (disinterested = impartial)   5. principal

Exercise 46
1. passed   2. was   3. pushed, was   4. were   5. looked   6. overflowed   7. stayed, talked, went   8. was

Exercise 47
1. We   2. A light fall of snow (*or simply* fall)   3. A faint sun (*or* sun)   4. brown earth and dark grass   5. spring

Exercise 48
1. am   2. married, was, came, was, was   3. didn't move, was   4. had moved, would have meant   5. Has been   6. would have suited   7. should have felt   8. can (survive)   9. am, is, think   10. is

Exercise 49
1.   The two prisoners/   2. The Bishop/
3.   The Mayor, a great bull of a man with angry eyes,/
4.   such a strange pair / could have come together how?
5.   The General's face /

Exercise 50
1. a few empty bottles (*or simply* bottles)   2. his knee   3. that colour   4. his tea   5. the South Atlantic   6. that   7. That   8. What   9. Which   10. Whose letter (*or* letter)

Exercise 51
1. intransitive 2. transitive 3. transitive 4. intransitive 5. intransitive 6. intransitive 7. transitive 8. transitive 9. intransitive 10. transitive 11. intransitive

Exercise 53
1. him 2. them 3. the dog 4. me 5. them

Exercise 54
(Note that the verb is *not* part of the complement: the complement completes the sense of the verb.)
1. his birthday 2. friendly 3. informer 4. experts 5. our first choice 6. the last to arrive 7. the capital of Lichtenstein 8. What (In questions, the normal order of sentences is often reversed. In this question, the logical subject of *is* is *the capital of Luxembourg*, and so *What* is the complement.)

Exercise 55
1. are (but *is* would be acceptable) 2. was 3. was 4. are 5. is 6. was 7. was 8. gives 9. remembers 10. was 11. are 12. were (but *was* would not be wrong) 13. was 14. is 15. was 16. are 17. phones 18. are (but better recast: My colleagues are not going on holiday, nor am I.)

Exercise 56
Numbers 3, 4 (present tense, but denoting future), 5 (ditto), 7, 9. (Sentence 10 is not in the present tense, despite the word *now*; in the context *now* means *at that time*.)

Exercise 57
Numbers 1, 2, 3, 4, 6, 7, 8, 9 (but *burst* can also be present)

Exercise 58
Numbers 1, 4, 5. Number 3 describes *present* intention to do something in the future.

Exercise 59
Simple Tenses:

Present	we write, they write
Past	we wrote, they wrote
Future	we shall write, they will write
Future in the Past	we should write, they would write

Continuous Tenses:

Present	we are writing, they are writing
Past	we were writing, they were writing
Future	we shall be writing, they will be writing
Future in the Past	we should be writing, they would be writing

Perfect Tenses:

Present	we have written, they have written
Past	we had written, they had written
Future	we shall have written, they will have written
Future in the Past	we should have written, they would have written

Exercise 60

had been boasting (past perfect continuous); had hunted (past perfect); am telling (present continuous); have seen ((present) perfect); declared (past (simple)); shall return (future (simple)); long (present (simple)); asked (past (simple)); had visited (past perfect); said (past (simple)); visited (past (simple)); shall be staying (future continouous); remember (present (simple)); happened, asked (past (simple)); will tell (future (simple)); answered, beamed (past (simple)); had gone (past perfect); had promised (past perfect); was making (past continuous); made, was, found, burst (past (simple)); are laughing (present continuous); said (past simple); am telling (present continuous).

Exercise 61

1. were angered (*subject*: residents *or* The local residents)   2. will be opposed (They)   3. have been told (you)   4. are being canvassed (shopkeepers)   5. Despite the sense of the sentence, the action of suffering is performed, not received, by the subject *I*; *can suffer* is active   6. have been warned (You)   7. active   8. was received (speech)   9. are shipped (gallons)   10. is similar to 5.

Exercise 62

1. The scene was lit up by the moon.
2. It will probably be taken by my neighbour.
3. The harvest may well be destroyed by the storm.

4. The letter was written by my wife.
5. A rest was taken by all of us . . . .
6. The instructions should be carefully studied by all the candidates.
7. He will be taught a lesson by that.
8. A short cut was shown us by a farmer.

Exercise 63
1. A mine *sank* the ship.
2. Small children can easily do this work.
3. All four choirs sang the choruses.
4. Council workmen began road works.
5. None of the prisoners spoke a word.
6. All present drank the toast.
7. Fifteen people swam the Channel last year.
8. All his friends forsook him.
9. His colleagues *sprang* a surprise on him.
10. The cat hid it.

Exercise 64
1. bidden   2. broadcast   3. borne   4. broken   5. ridden   6. eaten   7. laid   8. trodden

Exercise 65
1. subjunctive   2. indicative   3. indicative, infinitive   4. subjunctive, indicative, infinitive   5. imperative   6. subjunctive, indicative, infinitive   7. indicative, subjunctive   8. indicative, infinitive (i.e. (to) leave)   9. imperative, subjunctive   10. indicative, subjunctive

Exercise 66
1. non-finite, finite   2. non-finite, finite   3. infinite, finite   4. finite, finite   5. non-finite, finite, non-finite.

Exercise 67
(Many alternatives are possible.)
tiring game, boring book, interesting character, dying flower. working clothes, melting snow, gathering darkness, setting sun.

Exercise 68
(Many alternatives are possible.)
broken toy, furnished room, unexpected present, ruined building, uncut grass, stolen goods, heated liquid, chopped wood.

Exercise 69
steered, carried, committed, worn, done, won, written, been, had, woven, benefited, driven, begun, dug, eaten, found, held, shot, frozen, struck, spoken, sold, torn, read (i.e. same spelling but different punctuation, to rhyme with *bed*), crept, meant, thought, bought, left, bitten.

Exercise 70
1. winning (team)   2. fallen (leaves)   3. being (he)   4. overcome (she)   5. having been restored (painting)   6. having been restored (painting)   7. having been restored (painting)   8. No participle: *restored* is here a finite verb   9. lost (photographs)
10. having beaten (describes the understood *you*, the unstated subject of *mix*).

Exercise 71
(Several solutions are possible.)
1. Arriving late, we found that all the best seats had already been sold.
2. It being Wednesday afternoon, the shops were shut. (Absolute Construction)
3. While I was standing on the platform, a trolley ran over my foot.
4. When I banged the door, there was a complaint from upstairs.
5. Hoping to reduce his temperature, the doctor prescribed a new drug.
6. Since he had been regarded as a future Cabinet Minister his losing the election was a severe blow to his party.
7. The weather being wet *or* Since it was wet, I decided not to go.
8. As a result of the collision, a man appeared in court. (This solution avoids the participle altogether. Alternatively, but clumsily – Arising out of the collision, a

court appearance by a man took place. What does *arising* refer to? What *arose*? The appearance of a man in court.)

9. While not wishing to contradict, I believe (*or* I am of the opinion) that the difficulty could have been avoided.

10. After travelling all day, they will need a good night's rest.

Exercise 72

(1. Participle, describing *miners*)   2. striking (subject of verb *is*) 3. Hitting (subject of verb *is*)   4. drinking, driving (object of verb *mix*)   5. drinking (doing the work of a noun)   6. Drinking (subject of *is*)   (7. Participle, describing *water*)   In sentence 8, *having arrived* and *grounded* are both participles.

Exercise 73

Many answers possible. All clauses must include a finite verb.

Exercise 74

(Other answers possible)

1. which could be interpreted in two ways (an *ambiguous* remark)
2. which was not suitable for the occasion (an *inappropriate* outfit)
3. for which there can be no excuse (an *inexcusable* act)
4. from which there was no escape (an *inescapable* consequence)
5. who is always in a good humour (a *good-tempered* man)
6. where I was born (my *native* town)

Exercise 76

1. Emphasis on *first* syllable of noun, but *second* syllable of verb.
2. Ditto
3. Ditto
4. Noun rhymes with *bed*; verb rhymes with *feed*.
5. As for 1.
6. Ditto
7. Ditto
8. Ditto

Exercise 77

1. expresses futurity   2. expresses determination   3. expresses

futurity 4. expresses willingness 5. expresses futurity 6. expresses determination (means *I will not*) 7. expresses futurity 8. expresses determination.

Exercise 79

was sounded:	subject *trumpet:*	no object (verb is passive)
were thrown:	subject *doors:*	no object (verb is passive)
scampered:	subject *attendant:*	no object (verb is intransitive)
waited:	subject *we:*	no object (verb is intransitive)
happened:	subject *nothing:*	no object (verb is intransitive)
crept:	subject *attendant:*	no object (verb is intransitive)
peered:	subject *attendant:*	no object (verb is intransitive)
whistled:	subject *he:*	no object (verb is intransitive)
waved:	subject *he:*	object *cap*
began:	subject *he:*	object *to leap* (see section 13 (*a*))
passed:	subject *minutes:*	no object (verb is intransitive)
happened:	subject *nothing:*	no object (verb is intransitive)
walked:	subject *bull:*	no object (verb is intransitive)
looked:	subject *he:*	no object (verb is intransitive)
turned:	subject *he:*	no object (verb is intransitive)
found:	subject *he:*	object *doors*
began:	subject *he:*	object *to graze*
had:	subject *he:*	object *conception*
was expected:	subject *what:*	no object (verb is passive)
wished:	subject *he:*	the object is an unstated *that* (*All* (*that*) *he wished*)
was:	subject *all he wished:*	no object (verb is intransitive)
came:	subject *it:*	no object (verb is intransitive)
put:	subject *he:*	object *fight*
was killed:	subject *he:*	no object (verb is passive)

Exercise 80
See answers to Exercise 79.

Exercise 81
1. to take, (to) have 2. to repair 3. no infinitive 4. enter (see section 11 (c)) 5. to have travelled 6. to be married 7. have helped (see section 11 (c)) 8. ring 9. work 10. have forgotten, to write

Exercise 82
1. coming, going, sitting, peering (participles)
2. walking (gerund), hovering (participle)
3. doomed, resigned (past participle)
4. climbing (participle)
5. sleeping, waking (gerunds)
6. Unmoved, seated (past participles)
7. whispering (gerund)
8. stumbling (gerund)
9. screeching (participle)
10. trotting, tinkling, stirring (gerunds); departing (participle)

Exercise 86
(Many possible answers)
1. rapidly 2. grumpily 3. hoarsely 4. soundly 5. generously

Exercise 89
(Several alternatives possible)
1. soon 2. now 3. finally 4. then 5. today

Exercise 90
(Several alternatives possible)
1. Here 2. abroad 3. everywhere 4. upwards 5. higher

Exercise 91
1. in a generous fashion
2. in good time
3. in that place
4. at a fast pace
5. for a long time

Exercise 92
1. if the weather permits 2. As summer approaches 3. as night was falling 4. where the river is deepest 5. before the week is over

Exercise 93
solemnly (adverb of manner); outside the booking office (phrase, denoting place); in black (phrase, denoting manner); in his hand (phrase, denoting place); then (adverb of time); as he

advanced (clause, denoting time); instantly (adverb of time); equally (adverb of manner); in a gloomy voice (phrase, denoting manner); as he handed his wreath to his neighbour (clause, denoting time); while he put his hand in his pocket (clause, denoting time); as he peered through the window at the dour faces (clause, denoting time); later (adverb of time); today (adverb of time).

Exercise 94
1. All the guests who arrived tucked in quickly.
2. The last person to come turned up at half past seven promptly.
3. In my view, he should have given the voters more opportunities of seeing him.
4. After we had had a swim, we managed to find somewhere to leave the car, with the help of a car-park attendant.

Exercise 96
smoothly, moodily, dramatically, callously, majestically, gaily, well, fast (i.e. same form for both adjective and adverb).

Exercise 97
momentarily, hourly, daily, sleepily (*or* asleep), lengthily (*or* lengthwise), heavenwards (*heavenly* is an adjective), sideways (*or* besides), ashore.

Exercise 98
1. homely, slovenly, sickly, etc.
2. Use an adverbial phrase: *in a homely way, in a slovenly manner*, etc.
3. *Timely* is one such. There are also words such as *agile* and *wily* which do have the adverbial forms *agilely* and *wilily*, but these are often avoided because of their sound.

Exercise 99
1. adjective 2. adverb 3. adverb 4. adjective 5. adverb 6. adjective 7. adverb 8, adverb 9. adjective

Exercise 100
sooner, more tenderly, more (*most* is the superlative form), oftener, more ill, further, faster.

Exercise 101
1. He plays the game merely for what he can get out of it. (The adverb *merely* belongs to the second part of the sentence.)
2. The country will remain a great world power only as long as its people work hard. (The country will not *only remain*: it will remain *only as long as . . . .*)
3. I was impressed by his manner rather than by what he said. (The original *rather impressed* gives the wrong impression. The intended sense is *I was impressed*, not *rather impressed*.)
4. As the sentence stands, the final phrase attaches itself to the preceding clause, giving the unintended meaning that he was finding fault without effect. The intended sense is that he was shot at without effect. The sentence should be recast: His secretary, with whom he was finding fault, shot at him, very fortunately without effect.
5. The word *only* is intended to apply to *this year*, not *joined*. Thus: He joined the club only this year.

Exercise 102
(Several alternatives are possible.)
1. fluently   2. reluctantly   3. carelessly, casually   4. intermittently   5. seldom, infrequently   6. humbly

Exercise 105
verb, noun, verb (infinitive), verb (present participle), noun, adverb, adjective, adverb, adverb, verb (present participle).

Exercise 106
adverbial, adjectival, noun (subject of verb *would help*), noun (object of verb *hear*), adverbial, adjectival.

Exercise 107
noun clause (object of *said*), adjectival clause (describing *countries*), adverbial (telling more about verb *brought*), adjectival (describing *places*), adverbial (telling more about verb *retire*), adverbial (telling more about *retire*).

Exercise 108

1. dread/hope; soundness/sickness; covetousness *or* gluttony/abstinence; humiliation/effrontery; setting out/arrival.

2. request/tell; protect/attack; stretch/contract; believe in/distrust; order/obey.

3. plentiful/scarce; suitable/inappropriate; loquacious/taciturn; pressing/leisurely; circumspect/imprudent.

4. quick/ly)/slowly; severely/amiably; satisfactorily/badly; cautiously/carelessly; initially/lastly.

Exercise 109

1. me 2. he 3. she 4. We 5. they 6. me 7. he

Exercise 110

1. It is not clear whom the second *she* refers to. If 'her sister', change *and she* to *who*. If not, delete the second *she* so that the subject of *returned* is quite clearly the first *she*.

2. Whose cure? Whose hands? One can reasonably guess that the cure is the patient's. As for the hands, say either *the patient's own hands* or *the doctor's hands*: the repetition is unfortunate, but clear.

3. Who is *he*? *Either* The manager, so he told his assistant, needed a holiday. *Or* The assistant, according to the manager, needed a holiday.

Exercise 111

1. It's 3. women's 4. There's

Exercise 112

1. pronoun 2. adjective 3. adjective 4. pronoun 5. pronoun 6. pronoun 7. adjective 8. adjective 9. pronoun 10. adjective 11. pronoun 12. adjective

Exercise 113

1. is 2. is 3. was 4. is 5. fly 6. risks 7. appeals 8. suits

Exercise 114

1. emphasising 2. emphasising 3. reflexive 4. reflexive 5. reflexive 6. emphasising

Exercise 115
We, One, himself, he, himself, we, him, He, each, us, him, This, we, it, ours, We, that (or could be regarded as adj. with noun unstated), somebody, we, we, We, ourselves, anyone, us.

Exercise 116
1. It was a poor game which was watched by only a small crowd.
2. The home team, whose supporters are highly critical, has had a poor season.
3. The visiting team, who (which) had had a mid-week match, looked very tired.
4. The referee, who was the object of many coarse comments, was kept very busy.
5. The captain of the home team, *whom* the crowd cheered whenever he got the ball, was the best player.
6. The referee made the decision, to which the crowd noisily objected, to abandon the match because of fog.

Exercise 117
1. whom   2. whom   3. who   4. whom   5. Whom

Exercise 118
1. Suddenly she stamped her foot, screaming at the same time, so that everyone could hear her.
2. She went to her bedroom, which was at the top of the house, leaving her husband downstairs.
3. Her husband, a nervous man who had the task of putting the cat out every night, was the only other occupant of the house.
4. The wall, to which a burglar alarm had been fitted, was exceptionally tall and covered with ivy.
5. The police, whose suspicions had already been aroused, soon arrived.

Exercise 119
1. we rented (that *or* which)
2. you want (whom)
3. he likes best (that *or* which)
4. No adjectival clause. *When you have read it* tells more about

the verb *return*, and is therefore adverbial – an adverbial clause of time.

5. the car made (that)
6. I was with (whom); she had ever seen (that)
7. No adjectival clause. *That you do not understand* is object of the verb *see* and is doing the work of a noun; it is therefore a noun clause, object of *see*.
8. we have just passed (*that* or which)

Exercise 122
1. who 2. which 3. whom 4. that 5. as 6. as 7. that 8. where.

Exercise 123
1. pronoun 2. adjective, pronoun 3. adjective, pronoun 4. pronoun, pronoun 5. Neither: *either* is an adverb here.

Exercise 124
(Several alternatives possible)
1. on 2. down 3. of 4. at 5. in.

Exercise 125
(Several alternatives possible)
1. through 2. behind 3. with 4. into 5. down, across, through, along.

Exercise 126
(*a*) 1. for (living) 2. near (us) 3. on (way)
(*b*) 4. of (collection) 5. with (whatever you choose) 6. in (What)
(*c*) 7. of (ruins) 8. in (street) 9. to (me) 10. near (where we parked yesterday)

Exercise 127
1. adverb 2. preposition 3. adverb 4. preposition 5. adverb 6. preposition 7. adverb 8. preposition

Exercise 128
1. me 2. him 3. me 4. Whom (object of preposition *with*) 5. Whom (object of preposition *with*) 6. Whom (object of verb *meet*) 7. Who (subject of *was*) 8. She 9. them, us

Exercise 129
1. contrary to the plans ... and *to* what was urged. (The word *contrary* should be followed by *to*, as it is in the early part of the sentence, and there is no reason for switching to *with* later.)
2. Delete *me* (or *To me*). One is redundant.
3. *different from*.
4. The ending is clumsy: Why do you want him to be written to?
5. Both *more preferable* and *preferable than* are wrong: Poverty with happiness is *preferable to* wealth with sorrow.

Exercise 130
(Several alternatives possible, but the following combinations are common.)
(*a*) 1. parody of 2. thirst for 3. suspicion of 4. bias against 5. heir to
(*b*) 6. full of 7. opposite to 8. dependent on 9. contemporary of 10. averse to
(*c*) 11. digress from 12. approve of 13. vie with 14. derive from 15. delve into

Exercise 131
1. for 2. of 3. with 4. to 5. on 6. over 7. of 8. in 9. by 10. with

Exercise 133
1. past 2. passed 3. past 4. passed

Exercise 134
1. preposition 2. preposition 3. adverb 4. noun 5. adjective

Exercise 135
1. adverb 2. preposition 3. adverb 4. adverb 5. preposition 6. preposition 7. adverb 8. preposition 9. adverbs 10. adverb, preposition, adverb, preposition

Exercise 136
(Many answers possible: the following are merely examples.)

(a)   Life has its ups and downs; He has a down on me; Let's walk over the downs.

(b)   The down train is not due for ten minutes.

(c)   They decided to down tools.

(d)   Put it down.

(e)   The brakes failed and the lorry careered down the hill.

Exercise 139
1. from   2. to   3. to   4. to   5. with

Exercise 140
1. single words   2. clauses   3. clauses   4. phrases   5. phrases

Exercise 141
1.   before (links two clauses: (*You must*) *Look* and *you leap.*)
2.   that (links two clauses: *It is quite clear* and *they are going to lose.*)
3.   if (links two clauses: *I'll come* and *I can.*)
4.   before (links two clauses: *The storm burst* and *we could find shelter.*)
5.   or (links two proper nouns, *Monday* and *Tuesday.*)
6.   *nor* (links two phrases: *by criticism in the press* and *by threats of legal action.*)

Exercise 142
(Several answers are possible.)
1.   . . . in winter, *but* robins . . .
2.   We cannot play tennis *because* the courts . . .
3.   . . . no friends, *nor* does he seem to want any.
4.   . . . to Christmas *because* we are going away . . . (not *when*, which would be a relative adverb. See Chapter 12, section 9.)

Exercise 143
(Several alternatives are possible.)
1. but   2. or   3. until   4. before   5. while   6. Although
7. that   8. unless

Exercise 144
1. conjunction   2. preposition (see Chapter 7, section 1)
3. preposition   4. conjunction   5. preposition   6. conjunction

Exercise 145
1. adverb 2. preposition 3. conjunction 4. adverb 5. preposition 6. conjunction 7. conjunction, adjective 8. pronoun

Exercise 147
(Many examples are possible.)
1. *I|They | A spokesman for the technical staff |* said that working conditions were unsafe.
2. Although *the health authorities* insisted that there was no cause for anxiety, the number of shoppers was much lower than usual.
3. The result was *a sharp reduction in the volume of trade.*
4. *This* being so, it was decided to close the premises.

Exercise 148
(Many examples are possible.)
1. He prepared *several different versions.*
2. It makes no difference to *us.*
3. She was trembling because she disliked *quarrels.*

Exercise 149
(Many examples are possible.)
1. His parents give *him* too much pocket-money.
2. Four *years'* work has been wasted.
3. *His* guess was right.

Exercise 150
1. Subjunctive mood, expressing a wish.
2. Verbal noun (gerund) acting as subject of verb.
3. Absolute construction.
4. Interrogative pronoun.
5. Pronoun in accusative after preposition.
6. Genitive of singular noun (short for *grocer's shop*).
7. Past participle, describing *they.*
8. Emphasising pronoun.
9. Relative pronoun referring to *car.*
10. Indirect object.
11. Adjective.

12. Present tense (but indicating future).
13. Present participle describing *speed*.
14. Adverb (of degree) describing adjective *inconsistent*.
15. Abstract noun.
16. Intransitive verb.
17. Adverbial phrase.
18. Reflexive pronoun.
19. Prepositions.
20. Conjunction.
21. Interjection.
22. Adverbial clause.
23. Comparative degree of adjective.
24. Gerund acting as subject of verb.
25. Adjectival clause (meaning *which he was driving*).

Exercise 151

1. Change *unless* to *except*. *Unless* is always a conjunction, not a preposition.
2. *Everyone* is singular. Therefore *has to bring his lunch and tea with him.*
3. *the likes of you and me.* The accusative *me* is necessary after the preposition *of*. Also the split infinitive can be easily avoided here: *to quarrel constantly* is better.
4. *the last*, not *the latter*, which can only be used of two (not four). Also *most* is needed instead of *more*, because the comparative *more* applies only to two.
5. The sentence goes adrift in the middle, and *which* has no verb: change to either ... *which, if (they were) implemented, would make the factory a happier place* or break the long sentence into two: ... *overlooked; if they were implemented, the factory would be a happier place.*
6. *laid.*
7. *all the brothers:* he is not one of *all his brothers*, and cannot therefore be the most attractive of a group to which he does not belong. Also *best-dressed* because *most well* is illiterate.
8. *my wife and me.* Just as one would naturally say *let me help*, one says *let my wife and me*: the insertion of *my wife* does not alter the accusative case of *me* after the verb *let*.

9. One chooses between x *and* y, not between x *or* y. Thus change *or* to *and* (and *chose* to *choose*).

10. *shall*, not *will*.

11. Omit *other*. For explanation, see 7 above.

12. A common error. Change *dislikes* to the plural *dislike*. The sense is that there are *men who dislike complaining* and *he* is not of their number.

13. *exulted*.

14. Unrelated participle. Either *Being co-directors, they all had to agree before a decision could be taken* or *Since they were co-directors, a decision could not be taken without the agreement of all of them*.

15. Change *very unique* to simply *unique* or to *very strange*, etc.

16. Either *It was at him that the blow was aimed* or *It was he at whom the blow was aimed.*

17. A bizarre picture. Retain one of the two metaphors (*top of the tree*, *plain sailing*) but do not mix both incongruously. *He has reached the top of the tree and can now expect no further struggles* or *He has succeeded in his profession and from now on he will have plain sailing*.

18. *centres on*. The popular expression *centres around* is nonsensical.

19. *While he was walking . . ..* Another unrelated participle.

20. Do not mix constructions in this way. Either use *one* throughout, or use *you* (*Surely you can behave as you like in your own home*) where *you* means *a man* or *any man*.

21. *who*. A common error. The nominative *who* is needed as subject of the verb *would get*. The *everyone hoped* is a sort of parenthesis: the grammar can be more clearly seen in *He is the man who (everyone hoped) would get the job*.

22. *Is either. Either* is singular. This assumes that only two shops are being referred to. If more than two are intended, either *Is any* or *Are any*.

23. Change *I and you* to *you and me*, the accusative *me* being necessary after the preposition *but*.

24. *None* is singular: change *are* to *is*.

25. *who*. See 21 for explanation.

Exercise 153

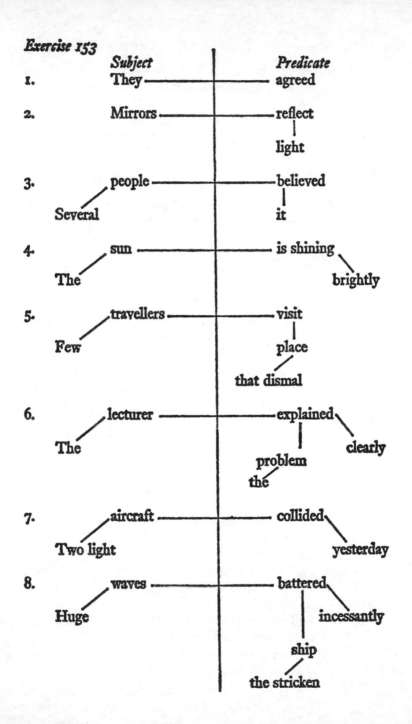

	Subject	Predicate
1.	They	agreed
2.	Mirrors	reflect / light
3.	people / Several	believed / it
4.	sun / The	is shining / brightly
5.	travellers / Few	visit / place / that dismal
6.	lecturer / The	explained / clearly / problem / the
7.	aircraft / Two light	collided / yesterday
8.	waves / Huge	battered / incessantly / ship / the stricken

Exercise 154

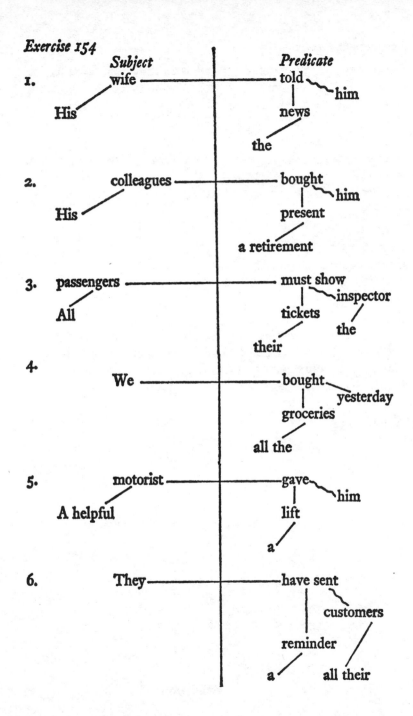

	Subject		Predicate

1. wife ——————— told ～ him
   His   news
                         the

2. colleagues ————— bought ～ him
   His   present
                         a retirement

3. passengers ———————— must show ～ inspector
   All   tickets   the
                         their

4. We ——————————— bought ～ yesterday
                         groceries
                         all the

5. motorist ————————— gave ～ him
   A helpful   lift
                         a

6. They ——————————— have sent
                                    customers
                         reminder   all their
                         a

(Note that the indirect object may have words describing it, and these follow the same rule as for adjectives describing other words in the sentence, i.e. the use of /.

Exercise 155
(Many answers are possible. The following are merely suggestions.)
1. (the) captain   2. chairman   3. scorer   4. (their) father   5. judge

Exercise 156
(Many answers are possible.)
1. calm   2. tiring   3. clear   4. early   5. warm

Exercise 157
1. complement   2. object   3. adverb   4. object   5. complement   6. object   7. complement   8. adverb   9. adverb   10. object   11. complement   12. adverb   13. complement   14. object   15. complement   16. adverb, complement.

Exercise 158

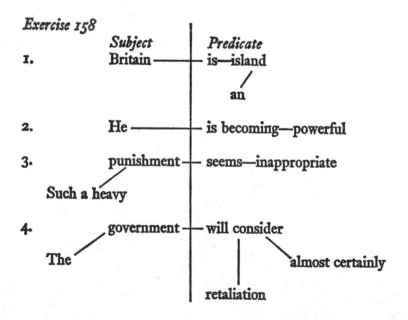

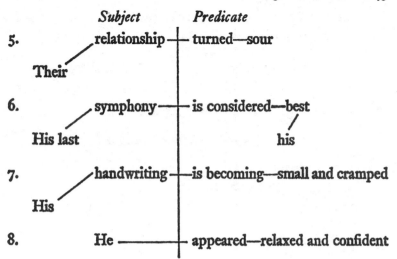

5. Their relationship — turned—sour

6. His last symphony — is considered—best / his

7. His handwriting — is becoming—small and cramped

8. He — appeared—relaxed and confident

Exercise 159

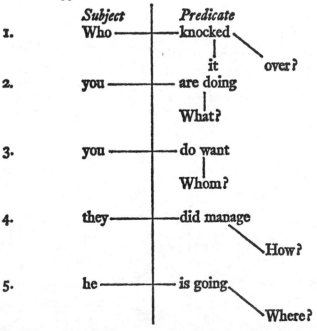

1. Who — knocked / it / over?

2. you — are doing / What?

3. you — do want / Whom?

4. they — did manage / How?

5. he — is going / Where?

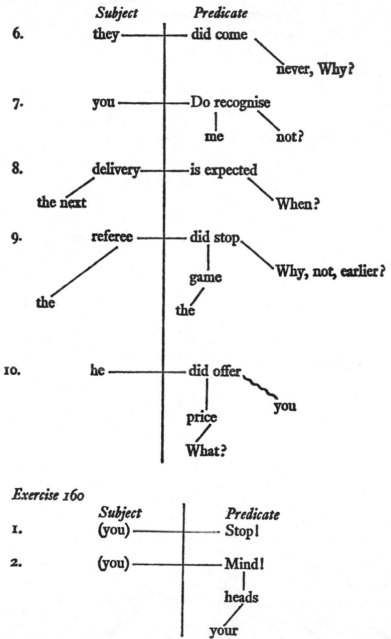

	Subject	Predicate
6.	they	did come

never, Why?

7.   you — Do recognise

me   not?

8.   delivery — is expected

the next   When?

9.   referee — did stop

game   Why, not, earlier?

the   the

10.   he — did offer

you

price

What?

Exercise 160

	Subject	Predicate
1.	(you)	Stop!
2.	(you)	Mind!

heads

your

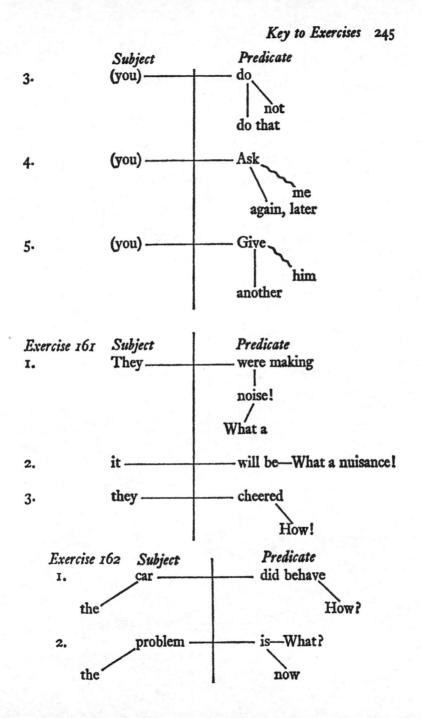

	Subject	Predicate
3.	(you)	do
		not
		do that
4.	(you)	Ask
		me
		again, later
5.	(you)	Give
		him
		another

Exercise 161

	Subject	Predicate
1.	They	were making
		noise!
		What a
2.	it	will be—What a nuisance!
3.	they	cheered
		How!

Exercise 162

	Subject	Predicate
1.	car	did behave
	the	How?
2.	problem	is—What?
	the	now

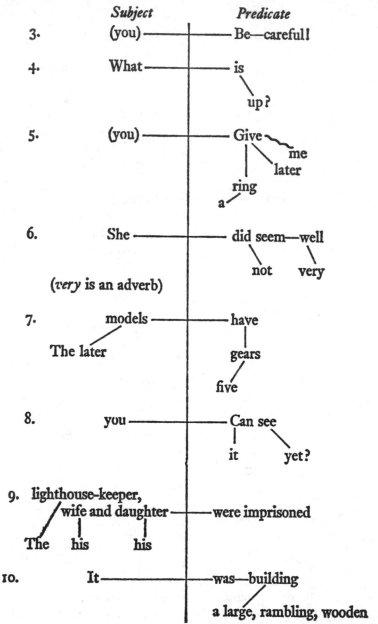

Subject		Predicate

3.   (you) —————— Be—careful!

4.   What —————— is
                       up?

5.   (you) —————— Give
                       me
                       later
                ring
              a

6.   She ————— did seem—well
                       not   very

(*very* is an adverb)

7.   models ————— have
      The later
                    gears
                five

8.   you ————— Can see
                it   yet?

9. lighthouse-keeper,
      wife and daughter ———— were imprisoned
   The   his   his

10.   It ————— was—building
              a large, rambling, wooden

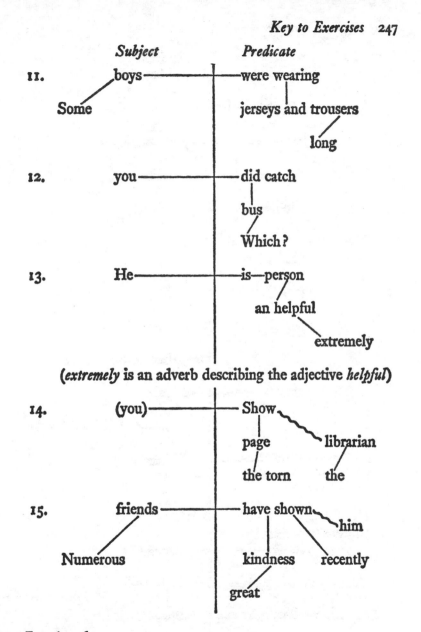

	Subject	*Predicate*

11. boys ——— were wearing
Some
jerseys and trousers
long

12. you ——— did catch
bus
Which?

13. He ——— is—person
an helpful
extremely

(*extremely* is an adverb describing the adjective *helpful*)

14. (you) ——— Show
page   librarian
the torn   the

15. friends ——— have shown
him
Numerous
kindness   recently
great

Exercise 164
1. my favourite author 2. an architect 3. the former Russian
capital 4. men of great experience 5. the mayor-elect

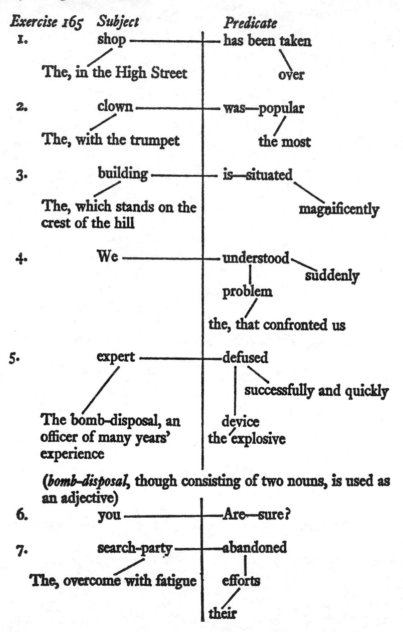

Exercise 165   Subject | Predicate

1.   shop —————— has been taken
     over
     The, in the High Street

2.   clown —————— was—popular
     the most
     The, with the trumpet

3.   building —————— is—situated
     magnificently
     The, which stands on the
     crest of the hill

4.   We —————— understood—suddenly
     problem
     the, that confronted us

5.   expert —————— defused
     successfully and quickly
     device
     The bomb-disposal, an   the explosive
     officer of many years'
     experience

     (*bomb-disposal*, though consisting of two nouns, is used as
     an adjective)

6.   you —————— Are—sure?

7.   search-party —————— abandoned
     The, overcome with fatigue   efforts
     their

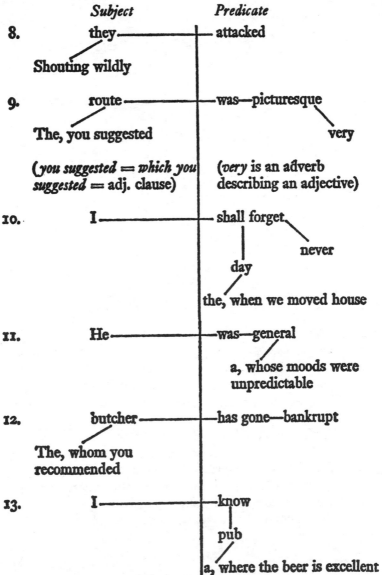

	Subject	Predicate
8.	they ———————	—— attacked
	Shouting wildly	

9. route ——————— was—picturesque

The, you suggested — very

(you suggested = which you suggested = adj. clause)　　*(very is an adverb describing an adjective)*

10. I ——————— shall forget

never

day

the, when we moved house

11. He ——————— was—general

a, whose moods were unpredictable

12. butcher ——————— has gone—bankrupt

The, whom you recommended

13. I ——————— know

pub

a, where the beer is excellent

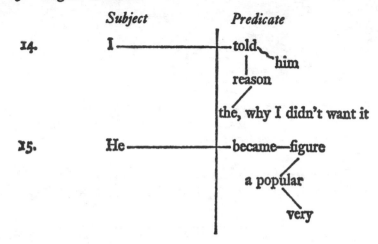

          Subject   Predicate
14.   I────────────────────────│────told
                                    │   him
                                    │   reason
                                    the, why I didn't want it

15.   He───────────────────────│────became─figure

                                    a popular

                                         very

Exercise 166
(Several answers are possible.)
1. In what/which place?   2. In what manner?   3. For what
reason?

Exercise 167
(Many answers are possible.)
1 *a.*   The fugitives ran off round the corner.
  b.   The shop round the corner opens on Sundays.
2 *a.*   Children are playing in the street.
  b.   The water-main in the street has burst.
3 *a.*   The boxer retired with a broken nose.
  b.   The boxer with a broken nose was forced to retire.
4 *a.*   The search-party spread out across the fields.
  b.   The path across the fields is becoming overgrown.
5 *a.*   Please put it near the wall.
  b.   The plants near the wall don't get enough sun.

Exercise 168

          Subject   Predicate
1.   visitors───────│───drove

     The   away

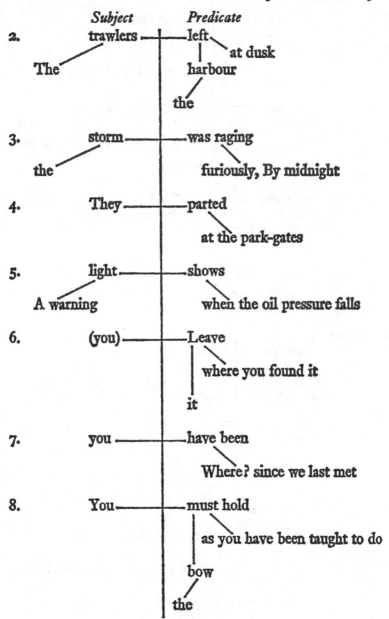

| | *Subject* | *Predicate* |

2. The trawlers — left
   at dusk
   harbour
   the

3. the storm — was raging
   furiously, By midnight

4. They — parted
   at the park-gates

5. A warning light — shows
   when the oil pressure falls

6. (you) — Leave
   where you found it
   it

7. you — have been
   Where? since we last met

8. You — must hold
   as you have been taught to do
   bow
   the

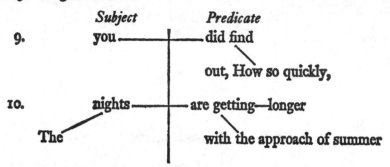

```
         Subject              Predicate
9.      you _____|_____ did find

                    |          out, How so quickly,

10.       nights ___|___ are getting—longer
      The                    with the approach of summer
                    |
```

Exercise 169
1. what your opinion is   2. that he is guilty   3. when he is
expected to arrive   4. how the problem can be solved   5. if he
knows the way *or* what the way is

Exercise 170
1. the date of a general election   2. the time   3. (the location
of) the best grazing   4. the working of the drains   5. their
friends' hiding-place

Exercise 171

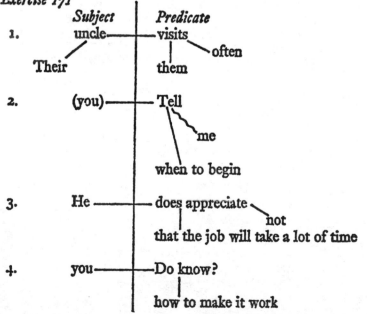

```
         Subject         Predicate
1.      uncle _____|____ visits
      Their          |        ↘ often
                     them

2.      (you) _____|____ Tell
                            ↘ me
                     when to begin

3.      He _____|____ does appreciate ↘
                     |                    not
                     that the job will take a lot of time

4.      you _____|____ Do know?
                     |
                     how to make it work
```

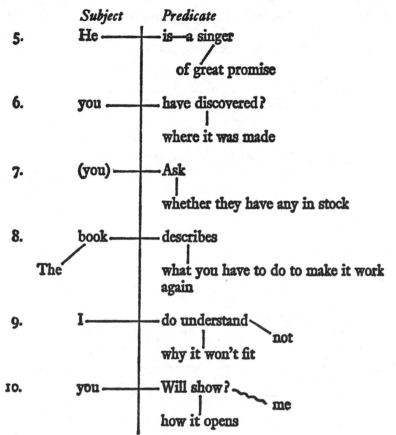

	Subject	Predicate

5. He — is—a singer
of great promise

6. you — have discovered?
where it was made

7. (you) — Ask
whether they have any in stock

8. book — describes
The
what you have to do to make it work again

9. I — do understand ~ not
why it won't fit

10. you — Will show? ~ me
how it opens

Exercise 173
1. adverbial clause (telling where the main verb *put* takes place)
2. Noun clause (object of *show*)
3. adjectival clause (describing *place*)
4. adjectival clause (describing *reason*)
5. noun clause (object of *claimed*)
6. adverbial clause (telling when the main verb *shone* takes place)
7. adjectival clause (describing *time*)
8. noun clause (object of *know*)

9. adverbial clause (telling when the main verb *Look* takes place)
10. adjectival clause (describing *week*)

Exercise 174
1. adverbial (time); adverbial (place)
2. adverbial (manner)
3. noun phrase (subject of verb); adverbial; noun phrase (after preposition *from*)
4. adjectival (describing *fog*); noun phrase (object of verb)
5. noun phrase in apposition to *Nelson*; adverbial (manner)

Exercise 175
1. which were (had been) placed below the water-line (adj. clause describing *lights*)
2. that there was a leak in the boiler (noun clause object of *reported*)
3. where the lake was deepest (adverbial clause of place)
4. that there were numerous faults in the mechanism (noun clause object of *revealed*)
5. when the storm was at its height (adverbial clause of time)

Exercise 177
at hand, by hand, from hand, to hand, from hand to mouth, in hand, on one's hands, on the other hand, out of hand, with a heavy hand (etc.)

Exercise 179
(Many answers possible)
1. To arrive punctually is better than being late.
2. We want to arrive punctually.
3. The aim must be to arrive punctually.

Exercise 181
(Many answers possible)
1 *a.* Do you know when the tide turns?
  b. They will put to sea when the tide turns.
  c. The time when the tide turns is different every day.
2 *a.* Can you tell me where it can be found?
  b. Put it where it can be found.
  c. Put it in a place where it can be found.

Exercise 182

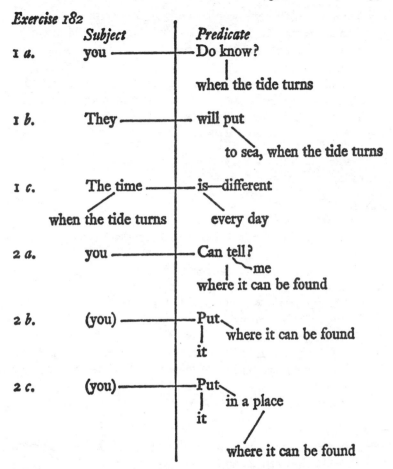

Exercise 183
1. I beg your pardon   2. I am sorry   3. Smoking is forbidden
4. If there are more, things will be merrier   5. Please let me see
your tickets   6. Scotland Yard are conducting a new probe
7. A director has been sacked   8. There is a price reduction of
seventy-five pence   9. There is a dual carriageway ahead of you
10. What did you say? *or* What do you mean? *or* I can't believe
what you say (etc.).

Exercise 184
1.   I knocked twice but received no answer.

2.   The policeman held up his hand and the traffic stopped.
3.   The policeman held up his hand but the traffic did not stop.
4.   The river burst its banks and flooded the neighbouring fields.
5.   He did not come, nor did his wife. (*not* He and his wife did not come, *which is a simple sentence with a double subject.*)
6.   You must hurry or you will be late.

Exercise 185
1. Double   2. Simple   3. Simple   4. Simple   5. Double   6. Multiple   7. Double   8. Multiple

Exercise 186
1.   The match was held up because of a violent thunderstorm.
2.   Owing to the intense heat, several spectators fainted.
3.   All his schemes failed.
4.   I was too astonished to speak.
5.   She is a gifted pianist with many admirers.
6.   Although losing heavily at half-time, they eventually won, to everyone's surprise.
7.   Having become a man, I have put away childish things.
8.   People laughed at him because of his unconventional dress.
9.   The pumps will have to be repaired to prevent further losses.
10.   Neither he nor his wife came.

Exercise 187
(The main clause is given in each case. The rest of each sentence constitutes an adjectival clause.)
1.   He is very careful of his appearance
2.   His sister-in-law has never married
3.   The room was empty
4.   The candidates were assembled in the room
5.   He had small hands
6.   Can you explain the reason
7.   She lived alone with her mother
8.   It dates from the time
9.   He is an actor
10.   They had the same trouble

Exercise 188

1. No adjectival clause: *why he phoned* does not describe a noun or pronoun in the main clause.
2. (that) he told
3. (which) he is writing
4. (that) they called at
5. (whom) you recommended
6. No adjectival clause: here *where* introduces an adverbial clause.
7. when nothing seemed to go right.
8. No adjectival clause: here *when* introduces an adverbial clause.

Exercise 189

1. adjectival 2. co-ordinate 3. adjectival 4. adjectival (short for *when war broke out*) 5. co-ordinate 6. co-ordinate 7. adjectival 8. co-ordinate

Exercise 190

1. In her hair she wore jewels which her husband had bought her.
2. We stopped for petrol for about ten minutes.
3. A doctor gave him some medicine that was distinctly unpleasant.
4. . . . a fine carriage which was drawn by two white horses and which had red wheels.
5. The Management may refuse admission as it considers proper.
6. . . . a book which deals . . .
7. *Delete* and
8. *Delete* and
9. *This sentence is correct.*
10. . . . which is over three hundred years old and which is now . . . .

Exercise 191

1. as they had made previously
2. as no-one had ever experienced before

3. as I was operated on (*correct to* by whom I was operated on *or* who operated on me)
4. as we did last year (*correct to* to which we went last year *or* which we visited last year)
5. as he was yesterday (*correct to* in which he was yesterday *or* as he was in yesterday)

Exercise 192
1. after the crowds had left
2. when the sun is at its hottest
3. Before he retired
4. since they were first laid out
5. while I reach into the corner
6. as long as you like
7. *No adverbial clause*
8. As soon as the final whistle sounded

Exercise 193
1. adverbial   2. adverbial   3. adjectival   4. adjectival   5. adjectival   6. adverbial   7. adverbial (but not a clause of time. See next section)   8. adverbial

Exercise 194
1. wherever it's convenient (adverbial)
2. where it was made (adjectival)
3. *No dependent clause*
4. where I bought it (*not adjectival, because it describes no noun, and not adverbial clause of place, because it does not say where the remembering took place. See section on noun clauses.*)
5. where the cat can't get at it (adverbial)
6. where the waters are calmer (adjectival)
7. where no man has been before (adverbial)
8. wherever they looked (adverbial)

Exercise 195
1. as they had never worked before
2. as I showed you
3. as if his life depended on it
4. than he appears to be

5. than had at first been feared
6. as though nothing had happened

Exercise 196

1 *a.* ... more than they visit us.
  b. ... more than we visit their families.
2 *a.* ... than he does.
  b. ... than I do about him.
3 *a.* ... than I write to them.
  b. ... than they write to her.

Exercise 197

1. because there is a strike at the ports
3. As the speech was ending *is an adverbial clause of time.*
4. Seeing that the ground is uneven
5. since all other means of escape were blocked
6. *No subordinate clause.*
7. Since I last saw him *is an adverbial clause of time.*
8. in that the corridors were too narrow

Exercise 202

1. that government intervention is inevitable
2. that first-time buyers cannot afford them
3. so that the ferry could not leave
4. *Adverbial clause of purpose.*
5. *No adverbial clause.*
6. that no-one can understand it

Exercise 204

1. if it's convenient
2. *No clause of condition.*
3. if we have their full co-operation
4. Unless we have their full co-operation
5. Provided we have their full co-operation
6. Were we to have their full co-operation
7. Should he arrive (while I'm out *is a subordinate adverbial clause of time*)
9. on condition that we're allowed to pay our way
9. Had I not enquired
10. If taxes were lowered

11.   *Adverbial clause of concession.*
12.   if I will

Exercise 206
1 *a.*   Implies that he has or could have witnesses.
  b.   Implies that he does not have witnesses.
2 *a.*   Implies that the 'if' clause represents a possibility.
  b.   Implies that the 'if' clause represents an impossibility.
3 *a.*   Implies that the conditional clause could become a fact.
  b.   Implies that the conditional clause is not a fact.

Exercise 207
as the only guard was over eighty (Reason, *thought*); so that he could become friendly with the keeper (Purpose, *made*); that he persuaded the keeper to allow his daughter to marry Blood's 'nephew' (Result, *was successful*); when the old man came into the Tower with his daughter for the wedding ceremony (Time, *was seized*); while one snatched at the crown (Time, *took*); since the latter was too long to be carried inconspicuously (Cause, *was sawn*); as they were busily engaged in stowing away the booty (Time, *came*); although they could have overpowered the youth (Concession, *ran*); as they were making their way across St Catherine's Wharf (Time, *were caught*); if King Charles had listened to his advisers (Condition, *would have punished*); as he deserved (Manner, *did treat*); where other enemies of the State had been banished (Place, *did banish*); as Blood had been disappointed in his venture (Cause, *was given*); provided he mended his ways (Condition, *was given*).

Exercise 209
1.   noun clause in apposition   2.   adjectival
3.   noun clause in apposition   4.   adjectival (*that we have to face*)
5.   adjectival   6.   adjectival
7.   noun clause in apposition   8.   (noun clause subject)

Exercise 213
(Many answers are possible.)
1.   . . . what he is.

2. . . . what(ever) you like.
3. . . . what it is *or* what it has become.

Exercise 215

1. that they would travel by train together (Noun clause object of *decided*)
2. *No noun clause*
3. that the carriage was warm (Noun clause subject, in apposition to subject-word *fact*)
4. What happened next (Noun clause subject of *was*)
5. that the ticket-collector was approaching (Noun clause object of *heard* in the adverbial clause of time)
6. that he had lost his ticket (Noun clause object of *discovered* in the adjectival clause)
7. what he was going to do to avoid paying again (Noun clause object of *asked*)
8. What he suggested (Noun clause subject of *was*)
9. what he proposed (Noun clause object of preposition *by*)
10. that he should hide under the seat (Noun clause object in apposition to the object word *idea*)
11. that this was a good idea (Noun clause object of *decided*)
12. That it was also a dirty one (Noun clause subject of *became*)
13. *No noun clause*
14. what you might have expected (Noun clause complement after *was*)
15. why there were five tickets for four passengers (Noun clause object of *asked*)
16. where their friend was travelling (Noun clause object of *revealed*)
17. that the seats were cleaner than the floor (Noun clause complement after *was*)

Exercise 217

1. When the war was over (adverbial clause of time qualifying found)
   who felt (adjectival clause qualifying *soldier*)
   that they deserved better (noun clause object of *felt*)

2. Unless there is a last-minute change of heart (adverbial clause of condition qualifying *will be made*)
that the factory is to be closed (noun clause in apposition to *announcement*)
which will be held next Monday (adjectival clause qualifying *news-conference*)

3. he gave (adjectival clause qualifying *reason*: means *that he gave*)
that demand had fallen (noun clause complement of *was*)
since colour-printing had been introduced (adverbial clause of time qualifying *had fallen*)

4. How such an accident could happen (noun clause subject of *will be investigated*)
when special safety measures were in operation (adjectival clause qualifying *period*)
- provided that proper co-operation will be available from the Yugoslavian government (adverbial clause of condition qualifying *will be investigated*)

Exercise 220

1. clause
2. multiple sentence
3. double sentence (The verbs are commands and have the force of main clauses. (See Chapter 1))
4. simple sentence (The words are elliptical for *There must be no parking*)
5. phrase
6. double sentence (See section 17 (*b*) above)
7. simple sentence (There is only one finite verb, and several phrases)
8. complex sentence

Exercise 221

		Clause	Kind	Function
1.	A	Daniel Defoe records an incident	Main	
	a¹	who wrote *Journal of the Plague Year*	Adjectival	Qualifies *Daniel Defoe* in A
	a²	which occurred at his brother's warehouse	Adjectival	Qualifies *incident* in A

Type: Complex

2.	A	he saw a woman coming out of the warehouse with some hats	Main	
	a¹	Whilst he was walking in Swan Alley	Adverbial of time	Qualifying *saw* in A

Type: Complex

3.	A	She told him	Main	
	a¹	that there were other people inside	Noun clause	Object of *told* in A

Type: Complex

		Clause	Kind	Function
4.	A	The fact made him suspicious	Main	
	a¹	that many people were leaving the warehouse with hats	Noun clause	In apposition to *fact* in A
	a²	that he went inside	Adverbial of result	Qualifying *made* in A

Type: Complex

5.	A	he asked the women	Main	
	a¹	When he had shut the gate behind him	Adverbial of time	Qualifying *asked* in A
	a²	what they were doing there	Noun clause	Object of *asked* in A

Type: Complex

6.	A	The truth was	Main	
	a¹	that they were seizing hats from the warehouse	Noun clause	Complement of *was* in A
	a²	which apparently had no owner	Adjectival	Qualifying *warehouse* in a¹

Type: Complex

7.

A	They thought	Main	
a¹	that they might take possession of them	Noun clause	Object of *thought* in A
a²	as no-one else was there to claim them	Adverbial of reason	Qualifying *take* in a¹

Type: Complex

8.

A	They were unconcerned and quiet	Main	
a¹	as if they had been at a shop	Adverbial of manner	Qualifying *were* (*unconcerned*) in A

Type: Complex

Exercise 222

(Various combinations are possible.)

1. At the beginning of each session, Parliament is opened by the Sovereign, who outlines the schemes which will be debated by Parliament.
2. Representatives, who are known as MP's and come from every part of the country, are elected to Parliament by the people.
3. Debates, which are sometimes noisy, are under the control of the Speaker, who has to be impartial.
   The policy of the Government is directed by the Prime Minister, who is assisted by the Cabinet, each member of which is responsible for one State Department.

Exercise 223

		Clause	Kind	Function
1.	A	The ambulance arrived quickly	Main	
	B	but it was too late	Main	Co-ordinate with A

Type: Double

		Clause	Kind	Function
2.	A	They searched	Main	
	B	and (they) searched	Main	Co-ordinate with A
	C	and finally (they) found it	Main	Co-ordinate with A and B

Type: Multiple

		Clause	Kind	Function
3.	A	I know (him)	Main	
	B	and (I) like him	Main	Co-ordinate with A
	C	but few others do	Main	Co-ordinate with A and B

Type: Multiple

		Clause	Kind	Function
4.	A	The countryside was dry and parched	Main	
	B	and little farming is possible	Main	Co-ordinate with A
	a^1	through which we passed	Adjectival	Qualifying *countryside* in A

Type: Double

		Clause	Kind	Function
5.	A	The winning team returned to their home town	Main	
	B	and were given a civic reception	Main	Co-ordinate with A
	a¹	after the game was over	Adverbial of time	Qualifies *returned* and *were given* in A and B
	b¹	because they had brought home the cup for the first time	Adverbial of reason	Qualifies *were given* in B

Type: Double

		Clause	Kind	Function
6.	A	An inspector poked his head through the window	Main	
	B	and informed us	Main	Co-ordinate with A
	b¹	that a minor fault had occurred	Noun clause	Object of *informed* in B
	b²	and (that)there would be a delay	Noun clause	Object of *informed* in B
	b³	until it was repaired	Adverbial of time	Qualifying *would be* in b²

Type: Double

Exercise 224

		Clause	Kind	Function
1.	A	He consulted a timetable	Main	
	B	and found that there was a train	Main	Co-ordinate with A
	b¹	which would get him to Crewe	Adjectival	Qualifying *train* in B
	b²	before the wedding was due to start	Adverbial of time	Qualifying *get* in b¹

Type: Double

2.	A	That day a blizzard overtook them with such violence	Main	
	a¹	that the leader realised	Adverbial of result	Qualifying *overtook* in A
	a²	(that) no-one could survive in such fury	Noun clause	Object of *realised* in a¹

Type: Complex

3.

A	No-one could predict	Main	
a¹	how the war would spread	Noun clause	Object of *predict* in A
a²	or how long it would last	Noun clause (co-ordinate with a¹)	Object of *predict* in A
a³	or how it would end	Noun clause (co-ordinate with a¹ and a²)	Object of *predict* in A

Type: Complex

4.

A	The boys were so closely alike	Main	
a¹	that no-one could identify them	Adverbial of result	Qualifying *were* (*alike*) in A
a²	if he tried	Adverbial of condition	Qualifying *could identify* in a¹

Type: Complex

5.

A	It is uncertain	Main	
a¹	how things will end	Noun clause	In apposition to *It* in A

Type: Complex

6.	A	Despite expectations, the divorce rate is now so high	Main	
	a¹	that a Royal Commission is likely to be announced	Adverbial of result	Qualifying *is* in A
	a²	that it would soon stabilise	Noun clause	In apposition to *expectations* in A
	a³	when Parliament resumes	Adverbial of time	Qualifying *announced* in a¹

Type: Complex

7.	A	A television director controls the cameras by means of the headphones	Main	
	B	and personally decides	Main	Co-ordinate with A
	a¹	(which) each cameraman wears	Adjectival	Qualifying *headphones* in A
	b¹	which shots he will use	Noun clause	Object of *decides* in B

Type: Double

8.	A	Everyone has some experience of failure	Main	
	B	and an honest record of (it) is the chief merit of this short story, published last week	Main	Co-ordinate with A
	b¹	how it feels	Noun clause	Object of preposition *of* in B

Type: Double

		Clause	Kind	Function
9.	A	Two nouns are said to be in· apposition	Main	
	a¹	when they are similar in meaning	Adverbial of time (or condition)	Qualifying *are said* in A
	a²	and (when they) are identical in grammatical function	Adverbial of time or (condition) co-ordinate with a¹	Qualifying *are said* in A

Type: Complex

10.	A	He was sitting up in bed	Main	
	B	and (he was) rocking from side to side	Main	Co-ordinate with A
	C	but at the sight of me his hands dropped from the reins	Main	Co-ordinate with A and B
	D	and (his hands) lay quiet	Main	Co-ordinate with A B and C
	b¹	as though he were riding a horse	Adverbial of manner	Qualifying (*was*) *rocking* in B

Type: Multiple

11.	A	Refrigerated ships now bring meat from South America	Main	
	B	and it is now worthwhile . . . (rest of sentence)	Main	Co-ordinate with A
	a¹	that is no dearer than English fresh meat	Adjectival	Qualifies *meat* in A

Type: Double

12.	A	Shakespeare's theatre did well	Main	
	B	but it could not survive on his plays alone	Main	Co-ordinate with A
	b¹	because the plays ran for only short periods	Adverbial of reason	Qualifying *survive* in B
	b²	(because) the repertory had to be large	Adverbial of reason (co-ordinate with b¹)	Qualifying *survive* in B
	b³	and (because) capricious audiences had to be given variety	Adverbial of reason (co-ordinate with b¹ and b²)	Qualifying *survive* in B

Type: Double

		Clause	Kind	Function
13.	A	His state of weakness was such	Main	
	B	he was consumed by fever	Main	Co-ordinate with A
	C	and he would have died but for the attention of his friends	Main	Co-ordinate with A and B
	a^1	that he was unable to digest any food	Adverbial of result	Qualifying *was* in A
	c^1	who rescued him from the excesses	Adjectival	Qualifying *friends* in C
	c^2	into which he had been throwing himself	Adjectival	Qualifying *excesses* in c^1

Type: Multiple

14.	A	It is obvious	Main	
	B	and it is ridiculous to pretend	Main	Co-ordinate with A
	a¹	that most of those ... do not go on to stronger drugs	Noun clause	In apposition to *It* in A
	a²	who smoke	Adjectival	Qualifying *those* in a¹
	b¹	that they do	Noun clause	Object of infinitive *to pretend* in B

Type: Double

15.	A	They climbed past a tethered goat and to a grassy place	Main	
	a¹	After they had eaten	Adverbial of time	Qualifying *climbed* in A
	a²	where the path led them	Adverbial of place	Qualifying *climbed* in A
	a³	from which they had a wide view of the harbour and the sea	Adjectival	Qualifying *place* in A

Type: Complex

		Clause	Kind	Function
16.	A	The invasion was not	Main	
	a¹	what it at first appeared to be	Noun clause	Complement of *was* in A
	a²	because the troops treated the inhabitants better	Adverbial of reason	Qualifying *was* (*not*) in A
	a³	than they had been led to expect	Adverbial of comparison	Qualifying *treated* in a²

Type: Complex

		Clause	Kind	Function
17.	A	They decided to draw lots	Main	
	a¹	so that there could be no allegations	Adverbial of purpose	Qualifying *decided* in A
	a²	that unfairness had taken place	Noun clause	In apposition to *allegations* in a¹

Type: Complex

		Clause	Kind	Function
18.	A	... is ...	Main	
	a¹	What is perhaps even more daunting	Noun clause	Subject of *is* in A
	a²	that starting to rebuild the city involves re-educating ... (rest of sentence)	Noun clause	Complement of *is* in A

Type: Complex

19. A	it is inevitable	Main	
a¹	Although they are clearly prepared to hold out	Adverbial of concession	Qualifying *is* in A
a²	for as long as is necessary	Adverbial of time	Qualifying *hold out* in a¹
a³	that the rebels must finally lose	Noun clause	In apposition to *It* in A
a⁴	because their numbers are fewer	Adverbial of reason	Qualifying *lose* in a³
a⁵	and (because) their supplies of food are increasingly low	Adverbial of reason (co-ordinate with a⁴)	Qualifying *lose* in a³

Type: Complex

		Clause	*Kind*	*Function*
20.	A	I have always felt very warmly, even nostalgically, towards the area	Main	
	a¹	because I was born there	Adverbial of reason	Qualifying *felt* in A
	a²	because I love the people	Adverbial of reason (co-ordinate with a¹)	Qualifying *felt* in A
	a³	and because I am immensely proud of its folk heritage, particularly of the enterprise of one grandfather ... and of the courage of another	Adverbial of reason (co-ordinate with a¹ and a²)	Qualifying *felt* in A
	a⁴	who was a prosperous silk merchant	Adjectival	Qualifying *grandfather* in a³
	a⁵	until he died at the age of 38	Adverbial of time	Qualifying *was* in a⁴
	a⁶	who walked 14 miles a day to work	Adjectival	Qualifying *another* in a³
	a⁷	until he was well into his sixties	Adverbial of time	Qualifying *walked* in a⁶

Type: Complex

Exercise 225
Common ones include B.B.C., T.U.C., C.B.I., H.M.S., E.E.C., A.A., U.N., C.I.D., B.A., F.B.I., I.Q. Most dictionaries list the most frequently used ones.

Exercise 226

in proper places.	emphasis.	purpose.
word order.	the best order'.	every word'.
check.	possible together.	in meaning.
kind gardener.	our minds.	

Exercise 227
(*a*) Commas after *Roche, statements, said, alone.* Full stop after *one.*
(*b*) Commas after *45* (optional), *it* (optional), *cult* (optional), *arts, drama.* Full stop after *process.* Commas after *ultimately, them.* Full stop after *nothing goes.* Commas after *ambition, aspiration, integrity.* Full stop after *mediocrity.* Commas after *for them* (optional), *educated.* Full stop after *person.* Commas after *suppleness, variety, ease, sentence, suspect.* Full stop after *spirit.* Commas before and after *indeed* (optional), after *writing, vehicle, language.* Full stop after *indifferent.* Commas after *approve, abet.* Full stops after *destroying it* and *civilisation.*

Exercise 228
1. Many English river-names are Celtic: Avon, Severn, Thames, Trent and Wye.
2. The subjects of the play are love, marriage, separation, and divorce.
   (Comma optional after *separation,* but it helps to climax the sentence in a way unnecessary in the previous sentence.)
3. All was peaceful in the park: ducks waddled, lovers strolled, children played, old men slept, and a few rowers plied their oars lazily.
   (Semi-colons would not have been wrong in place of commas, but the heavier punctuation of semi-colons would have produced an unwanted jerky effect.)

4.   The company has been making bricks for a hundred years; its expertise is thus very considerable.
5.   There was a sharp frost in the air; it cut the nose and lungs; you could feel your eyes water in the darkness. (Commas were sufficient for the list of short clauses in (3), but the longer clauses in this sentence require stronger punctuation, and there is not the same sense of having a list.)

Exercise 229
1.   . . . salt and pepper?
2.   . . . building!
3.   . . . could help.
4.   It won't cost much to replace – or so he says. (Or comma after *replace*.)
5.   You'll never guess what the price is – £17! (Or full stop after *is*.)
6.   The guide-book (a handsomely produced volume, incidentally) describes . . . Europe. (Commas or dashes would serve instead of brackets.)
7.   He doesn't understand why it won't start.
8.   I met a young American in Oxford Street on Monday. He told me he had seen all the productions of the Royal Shakespeare Company since Easter, and liked 'Coriolanus' best.

Exercise 230
1.   . . . to wash, iron and clean.
2.   The foreman said the manager does not know his job.
3.   A few miles on, the path is much worse.
4.   The policeman, says the burglar, is the bane of his life.

Exercise 231
1.   Full stop after *soon*, to emphasise *We miss you*. Semi-colon or colon both possible.
2.   . . . *comfortable, but the seats* . . . .
3.   Semi-colon after *tired*. A full stop would be too strong in view of the close relationship between the two statements, the second of which explains the first.
4.   Not a serious error; some would argue not an error at all,

Mary - Cruff

01764 655207

but *No* has the force of a complete sentence. Full stop, semi-colon or colon after *you*.

5. Full stop after *sooner*.
6. ... *the meat-thermometer, which is not the one I ordered.*

Exercise 233

'Ride into the town,' said the Squire, 'and see if there's a letter for me.'

'Yes sir,' said Andy.

'Do you know where to go?'

'To the town, sir.'

'Yes, but do you know where to go *in* the town?'

'No, sir.'

'Then why don't you ask?' said the Squire. 'Haven't I told you always to ask if you don't know something?'

Andy paused.

'Yes, sir,' he finally said.

'Then why didn't you ask?'

'Because I didn't want to be any trouble.'

The Squire couldn't help laughing at Andy's excuse for remaining in ignorance.

'Well,' he continued, 'you must go to the post-office.'

Index

Index

CREATIVE WRITING

DIANNE DOUBTFIRE

A lively and comprehensive handbook packed with practical advice for everyone with the urge to write.

This book looks at every form of writing — articles, short stories, poetry, plays, novels and non-fiction — and the different techniques of writing for adults or children, radio or TV. It offers clear guidelines for developing your talent and acquiring the basic craftsmanship which is the key to success. Dianne Doubtfire — established author, tutor and lecturer in creative writing — shares her experience and expertise to show how, given dedication and determination, you can not only improve your writing, but have the added satisfaction of seeing it in print.

TEACH YOURSELF BOOKS

CORRECT ENGLISH

B. A. PHYTHIAN

This practical guide and reference handbook will help you improve your own use of English in everyday life and enhance your appreciation of good English writing.

The book first provides handy summaries of the main rules of grammar and punctuation. It then examines some of the more common errors in spoken and written English, before giving practical advice on spelling and helpful definitions of words which are frequently confused and misused.

The second half of the book focuses on the correct and effective use of English in a wide variety of contexts, and illustrates the different types of language and style which contribute to the subtlety and variety of English expression. A particularly useful feature of the book is an extensive guide to the conventions of written English in everyday life, including business and commercial English, letters, reports, summaries and précis, and English for examinations.

TEACH YOURSELF BOOKS

LETTER WRITING

DAVID JAMES

This book is a complete guide to writing letters which say exactly what you want to say – and bring the desired response.

David James offers practical advice on the choice of layout, style and 'tone', and then examines different kinds of letters ranging from the simple thank-you note to the more involved job application or sales letter to a potential customer.

Numerous sample letters illustrate correct forms and common errors, and highlight the various conventions and courtesies observed in different parts of the world. Forms of address and a list of common abbreviations are also included for easy reference, making this a book for every home or office.

TEACH YOURSELF BOOKS

A selection of further titles
from Hodder & Stoughton / Teach Yourself

0 340 28765 9	Creative Writing	Dianne Doubtfire	£5.99	☐
0 340 42996 8	Correct English	B. A. Phythian	£5.99	☐
0 340 32441 4	Letter Writing	David James	£6.99	☐

All Hodder & Stoughton / Teach Yourself books are available from your local bookshop or can be ordered direct from the publisher. Just tick the titles you want and fill in the form below. Prices and availability subject to change without notice.

To: Hodder & Stoughton Ltd, Cash Sales Department, Bookpoint, 39 Milton Park, Abingdon, OXON, OX14 4TD, UK. If you have a credit card you may order by telephone – 01235 831700.

Please enclose a cheque or postal order made payable to Bookpoint Ltd to the value of the cover price and allow the following for postage and packing:

UK & BFPO: £1.00 for the first book, 50p for the second book and 30p for each additional book ordered up to a maximum charge of £3.00.
OVERSEAS & EIRE : £2.00 for the first book, £1.00 for the second book and 50p for each additional book.

Name ....

Address..

....

....

If you would prefer to pay by credit card, please complete:
Please debit my Visa / Access / Diner's Card / American Express (delete as appropriate)
card no:

Signature .... Expiry Date ....